THE ATTRIBUTES OF GOD

IN MODERN ENGLISH AND WITH A STUDY GUIDE

A. W. PINK

GODLIPRESS TEAM

© Copyright 2025 by GodliPress Team.

All rights reserved. The content contained within this book may not be reproduced, duplicated, or transmitted without direct written permission from the author or the publisher, except in the case of brief quotations embodied in critical articles or reviews.

Unless otherwise indicated, all Scripture quotations are from The ESV® Bible (The Holy Bible, English Standard Version®), © 2001 by Crossway, a publishing ministry of Good News Publishers. Used by permission. All rights reserved.

CONTENTS

About Our Revised Editions	v
Preface	vii
1. The Solitariness of God	1
2. The Decrees of God	8
3. The Omniscience of God	15
4. The Foreknowledge of God	22
5. The Supremacy of God	31
6. The Sovereignty of God	38
7. The Immutability of God	46
8. The Holiness of God	53
9. The Power of God	61
10. The Faithfulness of God	71
11. The Goodness of God	80
12. The Patience of God	86
13. The Grace of God	94
14. The Mercy of God	103
15. The Loving-Kindness of God	112
16. The Love of God	118
17. The Love of God for Us	126
18. The Wrath of God	134
19. The Contemplation of God	143
About A. W. Pink	151
Bibliography	153

ABOUT OUR REVISED EDITIONS

GodliPress exists to glorify God. While we respect the profound teachings of classic Christian authors, we do not necessarily endorse all their doctrinal views. Our mission is to faithfully preserve the rich theological depth and elegance of their works while making them more accessible to modern readers.

Our updated editions include:

- The unabridged, complete text, meticulously updated for clarity.
- Modern English sentence structure and vocabulary.
- Updated organization and headings for easier navigation.
- Scripture references from the English Standard Version (ESV).

- A thoughtfully crafted Study Guide for deeper reflection and discussions.

The included Study Guide offers additional insights and thought-provoking questions designed to help you pause and reflect on what you've read, whether individually or in a group setting. It is not intended to add to or detract from the original message but rather to guide you in applying its truths.

Our hope and earnest prayer is that, through our carefully revised editions, you'll find these Christian classics easier to understand and apply. May God bless you richly through any teachings within these pages that align with the Gospel of Christ, as revealed in His inspired Word.

PREFACE

Now acquaint yourself with Him, and be at peace; Thereby good will come to you. —Job 22:21

Thus says the LORD: "Let not the wise man boast in his wisdom, let not the mighty man boast in his might, let not the rich man boast in his riches, but let him who boasts boast in this, that he understands and knows me, that I am the LORD —Jer. 9:23-24

A spiritual and saving knowledge of God is the greatest need of every person. The foundation of all true knowledge of God must be a clear mental understanding of His attributes as revealed in the Bible. An unknown God cannot be trusted, served, or worshiped.

In this book, an effort has been made to set out some of the principal attributes of God's character. If the reader is to benefit from reading these pages, they need to sincerely ask God to bless them, to apply His truth to their conscience and heart, so that their lives will be transformed in the process. Something more than a theoretical knowledge of God is needed. God is only truly known in the soul as we surrender ourselves to Him, submit to His authority, and bring all the details of our lives in line with His holy doctrines and commandments.

"Let us know; let us press on to know the LORD" (Hos. 6:3).

"If anyone's will is to do God's will, he will know" (John 7:17).

"The people who know their God shall stand firm and take action" (Dan. 11:32).

(A.W. Pink, 1930)

1

THE SOLITARINESS OF GOD

The title of this chapter is not clear enough to show its theme. This is partly because we are not used to meditating on the personal perfections of God. For those who only occasionally read the Bible, they are not aware of the awe-inspiring and worship-provoking grandeur of His divine character. It is commonly assumed that God is great in wisdom, wondrous in power, yet full of mercy. However, adequately understanding His being, nature, and attributes, as revealed in the Bible, is something that very, very few people manage. God is solitary and set apart in His excellency. "Who is like you, O Lord, among the gods? Who is like you, majestic in holiness, awesome in glorious deeds, doing wonders?" (Ex. 15:11).

Before Everything Else

"In the beginning, God" (Gen. 1:1). There was a time (if it can be called time) when God, in the unity of His nature (existing equally in three persons), was by Himself. There was no heaven, where His glory is now properly revealed. There was no earth to demand His attention. There were no angels to sing His praises, no universe to uphold by His power. There was nothing, no one, but God—not for one day, one year, or one age, but "from everlasting to everlasting" (Ps. 90:2). In eternity past, God was alone: self-contained, self-sufficient, and self-satisfied—needing nothing. If a universe, angels, or human beings were necessary to Him in any way, they also would have been called into existence from all eternity. Creating them when He did added nothing essential to God. He does not change (Mal. 3:6); therefore, His glory cannot be added to or taken away.

His Sovereign Will

God was not restricted, under any obligation, or required to create. He chose to do it purely as a sovereign act on His part, caused by nothing outside Himself, determined by nothing except His good pleasure because He "works all things according to the counsel of his will" (Eph. 1:11). He created everything simply for His glory. Do you think this is beyond what the Bible says? An answer can be found in the Law: "Stand up and bless the Lord your God from everlasting to everlasting. Blessed be your glorious name, which is exalted above all blessing and praise" (Neh. 9:5). God does not benefit from our worship. He did not need that external glory of His grace that comes from His people, because He is glorious enough in Himself without it. What made Him appoint His chosen to praise the glory of His grace? It was "according to the purpose of his will" (Eph. 1:5).

This is high ground we are walking into, new and strange to most readers, so it is good to move slowly. Let us look at the Bible again. Paul closes his long argument on salvation by pure and sovereign grace, then he asks, "For who has known the mind of the Lord, or who has been his counselor? Or who has given a gift to him that he might be repaid?" (Rom. 11:34-35). It is impossible to bring the Almighty under obligations to the creature—God gains nothing from us. "If you are righteous, what do you give to him? Or what does he receive from your hand? Your wickedness concerns a man like yourself, and your righteousness a son of man" (Job 35:7-8). It cannot affect God, who is blessed in Himself. "When you have done all that you were commanded, say, 'We are unworthy servants'" (Luke 17:10)—our obedience has profited God nothing.

We can go even further: Jesus added nothing to God in His essential being and glory, either by what He did or suffered. He manifested the glory of God to us, but He added nothing to God. He says so himself: "I have no good apart from you" (Ps. 16:2).

That whole Psalm is about Jesus. His goodness or righteousness reached His people (v.3), but God was above and beyond it all. Only God is the Blessed One (Mark 14:61). It is true that God is both honored and dishonored by men, not in His being, but in His character. It is also true that God has been glorified by creation, providence, and redemption. We do not dispute that. But all of this has to do with His glory and us recognizing it.

If God wanted to, He could have continued alone for all eternity without making His glory known to His creatures. Whether He should or not was up to Him. He was perfectly blessed in Himself before the first creature was made. And what about His creatures, what are they to Him? The Bible answers like this:

Behold, the nations are like a drop from a bucket,

and are accounted as the dust on the scales;

behold, he takes up the coastlands like fine dust.

Lebanon would not suffice for fuel,

nor are its beasts enough for a burnt offering.

All the nations are as nothing before him,

they are accounted by him as less than nothing and emptiness.

To whom then will you liken God, (Isa. 40:15-18)

This is the God of the Bible who is still "the unknown [God]" to most people (Acts 17:23).

It is he who sits above the circle of the earth,

and its inhabitants are like grasshoppers;

who stretches out the heavens like a curtain,

and spreads them like a tent to dwell in;

who brings princes to nothing,

and makes the rulers of the earth as emptiness. (Isa. 40:22-23)

How different is the God of Scripture from the one preached from the average pulpit?

The New Testament also agrees with the Old since they have the same Author!

Which he will display at the proper time—

he who is the blessed and only Sovereign,

the King of kings and Lord of lords,

who alone has immortality,

who dwells in unapproachable light,

whom no one has ever seen or can see.

To him be honor and eternal dominion. Amen. (I Tim. 6:15-16)

A God like this should be revered, worshiped, and adored. No one can match His majesty; He is unique in His greatness and peerless in His perfections. He sustains all but is independent of all. He gives to all but is enriched by none.

Through Revelation

A God like this cannot be found by searching. He can only be known as He is revealed to the heart by the Holy Spirit through the Word. Creation demonstrates a Creator so clearly that people are "without excuse" (Rom. 1:20), but we still agree with Job when he says, "Behold, these are but the outskirts of his ways, and how small a whisper do we hear of him! But the thunder of his power who can understand?" (Job 26:14). The apologist's argument for divine design has done much more harm than good, because it has brought the great God down to the level of finite understanding, and we have lost sight of His unique excellence.

The analogy used is of a rural person finding a watch and, looking at it closely, concluding there must be a watchmaker. So far so good. But what if that person sits down and tries to imagine this watchmaker—his emotions, manners, attitude, accomplishments, and moral character—all that make up a personality? Could he ever think or reason out a real man—the man who made the watch so that he could say, "I know him?" It seems useless to ask, but is it possible to grasp the eternal and infinite God with our human reason? No. The God of the Bible can only be known by those to whom He makes Himself known.

God also cannot be known by intellect. God is Spirit (John 4:24), and therefore, can only be known spiritually. But fallen man is not spiritual—we are carnal. We are dead to everything spiritual. Unless we are born again, supernaturally brought from death to life, miraculously translated out of darkness into light, we cannot even see the things of God (John 3:3), let alone understand them (1 Cor. 2:14). The Holy Spirit has to shine in our hearts (not minds) in order to give us "the knowledge of the glory of God in the face of Jesus Christ" (2 Cor. 4:6). And even that spiritual knowledge is partial. The born-again soul has to grow in grace and in the knowledge of the Lord Jesus (2 Pet. 3:18).

The main prayer and aim of Christians should be to "walk in a manner worthy of the Lord, fully pleasing to him: bearing fruit in every good work and increasing in the knowledge of God" (Col. 1:10).

Reflections

Pink does not just start off with this attribute by chance but selects it as the opening chapter for a reason. Like any good story, it sets the scene and the main character right from the beginning: God is God and there is no other like Him. Before Him, there was only Him! He was alone as God with no competition, rival, or colleague. The word solitariness simply means solitary, on His own, separated from all. In no way was he ever lonely as we might become when we are isolated. As a triune God, He was and is completely satisfied and content. This sets Him apart, not to be compared or linked with any other deities, since He was before all of them, and remains that way!

1. Where do other gods like Allah, Zeus, Baal, Ganesha, Vishnu, and Krishna fit into everything?
2. Is it arrogant of God to declare Himself the only one?
3. Why do you think God made people if He was not lonely?
4. Read Genesis 1:1. What does this say about God's origins?

2

THE DECREES OF GOD

The decree of God is His purpose or determination with respect to future things. We have used the singular form of purpose as the Bible does (Rom. 8:28; Eph. 3:11) because there was only one act of His infinite mind about future things. But we speak as if there were many because our minds are only capable of thinking of consecutive developments, as thoughts and circumstances happen, or referring to parts of His decree that seem to need a distinct purpose for each. But an infinite understanding does follow steps, going from one stage to the next: "Known to God from eternity are all His works" (Acts 15:18).

The Bible mentions the decrees of God in many verses, using different terms:

- The word "decree" is found in Psalm 2:7.
- In Ephesians 3:11 we see His "eternal purpose."

- In Acts 2:23, His "definite plan and foreknowledge."
- In Ephesians 1:9, the "mystery of His will."
- In Romans 8:29, He also "predestined."
- In Ephesians 1:9, His "purpose."

God's decrees are called His "counsel" to show they are incredibly wise. They are called God's "will" to show He was under no pressure and acting for His own pleasure. When a person's will determines their conduct, it is usually unpredictable and unreasonable. Wisdom is always associated with will when God acts, and so His decrees are called "the counsel of his will" (Eph. 1:11).

The decrees of God relate to all future events, whether they happened within time or were foreordained before time began. God's purpose was concerned with everything—great or small, good or evil. However, while God orders and controls sin, He is not the author of it, as He is the author of good. Sin cannot come from a Holy God by positive and direct creation, only by permission and negative action. God's decree extends to all creatures and events. It was concerned about our life and death, our state in time, and our state in eternity.

As God works all things in the counsel of His will, we learn about His counsel the same way we judge an architect's plan by inspecting the building erected under his direction. God did not simply decree to make man, place him on the earth, then leave him unsupervised. Instead, He set all the circumstances for every individual and all the particulars that make up the history of the human race from beginning to end. He did not just decree general laws for the government of the world, but He settled the application of those laws to all specific cases.

Our days are numbered, and so are the hairs of our heads. We can learn about God's decrees from His provision and the way He provides. His provision reaches the most insignificant creatures and the most minute events—the death of a sparrow, the fall of a hair.

Let us now consider some of the properties of the divine decrees.

They Are Eternal

To think they are made in time is to suppose that some new occasion has occurred, some unforeseen event, which has forced the Most High to come up with a new resolution. This would mean the knowledge of God is limited and that He grows wiser as time progresses—a horrible blasphemy. No one who believes God's understanding is infinite—past, present, and future—will ever agree to this false doctrine of progressive decrees. God is not ignorant of future events caused by human decisions. He has foretold them in many cases, and prophecy shows His eternal foresight.

The Bible confirms that believers were chosen in Christ before the world began (Eph. 1:4) and that grace was given to them (2 Tim. 1:19).

They Are Wise

Wisdom is shown in choosing the best possible ways and methods to accomplish them. We can see this from what we know of them. They are revealed in their execution, and every proof of wisdom in God's works is proof of His wisdom in the plan and conformity in how they are executed. "O Lord, how manifold are your works! In wisdom have you made them all" (Ps. 104:24). We only have a few examples to observe, but we can analyze them as we do with other cases and judge the unknown by what is known. Seeing the skill in how the parts of a machine work, we can naturally believe that the other parts are just as good. In the same way, we can be clear when doubts come in and block out any objections when we cannot discern what is good and wise. When we reach the limits of the finite and gaze toward the mysterious realm of the infinite, let us say, "Oh, the depth of the riches and wisdom and knowledge of God!" (Rom. 11:33).

They Are Free

Who has measured the Spirit of the Lord,

or what man shows him his counsel?

Whom did he consult,

and who made him understand?

Who taught him the path of justice,

and taught him knowledge,

and showed him the way of understanding? (Isa. 40:13-14)

God was by Himself when He made His decrees and was not influenced by any external cause. He was free to decree or not to decree, one thing and not another. We must credit Him who is supreme, independent, and sovereign in all His ways, with this freedom.

They Are Absolute and Unconditional

The execution of decrees does not depend on any condition. Each time God has decreed something, He has also decreed every method and way to make it happen. The One who decreed the salvation of His chosen people also decreed to work faith in them (2 Thess. 2:13). "My counsel shall stand, and I will accomplish all my purpose" (Isa. 46:10). That would not have happened if His counsel depended on a condition that might not be performed. But God "works all things according to the counsel of his will" (Eph. 1:11).

Side by side with the immutability and invincibility of God's decrees, the Bible teaches that people are responsible for their actions. If our thoughts are formed from God's Word, then holding onto one will not lead to the denial of the other. Of course, it is difficult to define where the one ends and the other begins. This is always the case where God and man coincide. Real prayer is composed by the Spirit, but it is also the cry of a human heart. The Bible is the inspired Word of God, but they were written by men who were instruments of the Spirit. Jesus is both God and man. He is omniscient, but "increased in wisdom" (Luke 2:52). He is almighty but was "crucified in weakness" (2 Cor. 13:4). He is the Prince of life, but He died. These are all mysteries, yet faith receives them without question.

Every objection against God's decrees finds problems with His eternal foreknowledge.

Jonathan Edwards said,

Whether God has decreed all things that ever come to pass or not, all that own the being of a God, own that He knows all things beforehand. Now, it is self-evident that if He knows all things beforehand, He either does approve of them or not—He either wills that they should be or not. But to will that they should be is to decree them (Edwards, 2024).

Finally, let us assume and look at the opposite.

To deny God's decrees means creating a world that is regulated by chance or blind fate. Then what peace, assurance, or comfort would there be for our poor hearts and minds? What refuge would there be to run to in difficult times? None! There would be nothing better than the black darkness and abject horror of atheism. How grateful we should be that everything is determined by infinite wisdom and goodness!

Praise and gratitude are due to God for His divine decrees. Because of them, "we know that for those who love God all things work together for good, for those who are called according to his purpose" (Rom. 8:28). We should say, "For from him and through him and to him are all things. To him be glory forever. Amen" (Rom. 11:36).

Reflections

Decrees, commands, declarations, directives, or announcements: God said it and it happened. In the very beginning, He commanded light, declared the heavens, directed animals, and announced the oceans. And He did not stop there... He continued to issue decrees. Like a king would set an order in motion, God simply dispensed His will into being. He spoke and it was. When we see the power of His words and His decrees, and that they are non-negotiable, non-returnable, and unbreakable, it opens our eyes to see that whatever He decides to do will be done, despite what we may see or feel. This is an incredible encouragement since we know He is true to His word.

1. What time limit is there on God's decrees?
2. If God is the maker and creator of everything, then did He create and decree sin?
3. What is God's eternal plan?
4. Read Philippians 1:6. What does this mean for us as Christians?
5. Where do we fit into God carrying out His decrees?

3

THE OMNISCIENCE OF GOD

God is omniscient. He knows everything: everything possible, everything actual; all events and all creatures, past, present, and future. He is perfectly acquainted with every detail in the life of every being in heaven, earth, and hell. "He knows what is in the darkness" (Dan. 2:22). Nothing escapes His notice, nothing can be hidden from Him, nothing is forgotten by Him. We can agree with the Psalmist, "Such knowledge is too wonderful for me; it is high; I cannot attain it" (Ps. 139:6). His knowledge is perfect. He never makes mistakes, never changes, never overlooks anything. "And no creature is hidden from his sight, but all are naked and exposed to the eyes of him to whom we must give account" (Heb. 4:13). Yes, this is the God "to whom we must give account"!

You know when I sit down and when I rise up;

you discern my thoughts from afar.

You search out my path and my lying down

and are acquainted with all my ways.

Even before a word is on my tongue,

behold, O Lord, you know it altogether. (Ps. 139:2-4)

What a wonderful being is the God of the Bible! Each of His glorious attributes should make Him honorable in our sight. His omniscience should make us bow in adoration before Him. But we do not meditate on this divine perfection much! Is it because thinking about it makes us uneasy? The fact is, nothing can be hidden from God! "I know what you are saying, for I know every thought that comes into your minds" (Ez. 11:5). Even though He is invisible to us, we are not invisible to Him. The darkness of night, the heaviest curtains, nor the deepest dungeon can hide sinners from His omniscient eyes. The trees of the garden could not hide Adam and Eve. No one saw Cain murder his brother, but his Maker witnessed the crime. Sarah might laugh derisively in the privacy of her tent, yet it was heard by Jehovah. Achan stole a bar of gold and carefully hid it in the ground, but God brought it to light. David took care to cover up his wickedness, but before long the all-seeing God sent one of His servants to say to him, "It was you!" And reminds us: "Be sure your sin will find you out" (Num. 32:23).

People would strip God of His omniscience if they could—proof that "the mind that is set on the flesh is hostile to God" (Rom. 8:7)! The wicked hate this divine perfection as much as they are forced to acknowledge it. They wish there might be no one to witness their sins, no one to search their hearts, no one to judge their actions. They want to banish such a God from their thoughts: "But they do not consider that I remember all their evil" (Hos. 7:2). Look at Psalm 90:8 —the logic has every Christ-rejecter trembling: "You have set our iniquities before you, our secret sins in the light of your presence."

But to the believer, God's omniscience is a truth that brings comfort. In times of confusion, we say, "But he knows the way that I take" (Job 23:10). It may be completely mysterious to me, quite incomprehensible to my friends, but "He knows!" When Christians are weak and tired, they reassure themselves, "For he knows our frame; he remembers that we are dust" (Ps. 103:14). In times of doubt and suspicion we can appeal to Him,

Search me, O God, and know my heart!

Try me and know my thoughts!

And see if there be any grievous way in me,

and lead me in the way everlasting! (Ps. 139:23,24)

When we fail and our actions contradict our hearts, our deeds deny our devotion, and we are confronted with the searching question: "Do you love me?", we reply with Peter: "Lord, you know everything; you know that I love you" (John 21:17).

This is an encouragement to prayer. There is no reason to be afraid that the prayers of the righteous will not be heard or that their sighs and tears will escape God since He knows the thoughts and intents of the heart. There is no danger of a

Christian being overlooked amongst all those who bring their petitions every day and night because God's infinite mind is capable of paying the same attention to millions as he is to one individual seeking His attention. Even if we do not have the appropriate language, or we struggle to express the deepest longing of the soul, it will not jeopardize our prayers because "Before they call I will answer; while they are yet speaking I will hear" (Isa. 65:24).

Past and Future

"Great is our Lord, and abundant in power; his understanding is beyond measure" (Ps. 147:5). God not only knows everything that has happened in the past in every part of His vast domains, and He is not only thoroughly acquainted with everything that is now taking place throughout the entire universe, but He is also perfectly aware of every event, from the smallest to the greatest, that will ever happen. God's knowledge of the future is as complete as His knowledge of the past and the present because the future depends entirely on Him. If it were possible for something to occur apart from God's permission, then that would be independent of Him, and He would immediately cease to be Supreme.

His knowledge of the future is not abstract, but something connected to and accompanied by His purpose. God has designed whatever it will be, and what He has designed must happen. As the Bible says, "he does according to his will among the host of heaven and among the inhabitants of the earth; and none can stay his hand" (Dan. 4:35). And also,

"Many are the plans in the mind of a man, but it is the purpose of the Lord that will stand" (Prov. 19:21). The wisdom and power of God are both infinite, so accomplishing whatever He has purposed is absolutely guaranteed. It is not possible for His counsel to fail in execution, just as it is impossible for the Trinity to lie.

Nothing relating to the future is uncertain so far as God's counsel is concerned. None of His decrees depend on creatures or secondary causes. There is no future event that is only a possibility or something that may or may not happen, because "known to God from eternity are all His works" (Acts 15:18 NKJV). Whatever God has decreed is 100% certain, because He does not change or shift like the shadows (Jam. 1:17). Therefore, we are told at the beginning of Revelations, which predicts so much of the future, of "the things that must soon take place" (Rev. 1:1).

The perfect knowledge of God is shown in every prophecy recorded in the Bible. In the Old Testament, we found many predictions concerning the history of Israel, which were fulfilled to the smallest detail, centuries after they were made. There are also many about the earthly ministry of Jesus, also fulfilled literally and perfectly. These prophecies could only have been given by God who knew the end from the beginning, established on the unconditional certainty of everything prophesied coming true. The Old and New Testaments contain other predictions about the future, and they also "must be fulfilled" (Luke 24:44) because they were foretold by Him who decreed them.

However, God's knowledge or awareness of the future is not a contributing factor. Nothing has ever come to pass, or ever will, simply because God knew it. The **cause** of all things is the **will** of God. The person who really believes the Bible knows that the seasons will continue to follow each other with consistent regularity to the end of history (Gen. 8:22), yet knowing this does not cause them to happen. So, God's knowledge does not come from things because they are or will be, but because He has **ordained** them to be. God knew and foretold the crucifixion of His Son hundreds of years before Jesus came to earth because God's purpose was that He was the Lamb slain from the foundation of the world. Jesus was "delivered up according to the definite plan and foreknowledge of God" (Acts 2:23).

Our Response

God's infinite knowledge should fill us with **amazement**. How much more exalted is the Lord than the wisest person! None of us knows what a day will bring, but His omniscient gaze sees everything that will happen.

God's infinite knowledge should fill us with holy **awe**. Nothing we do, say, or think, escapes His awareness. "The eyes of the Lord are in every place, keeping watch on the evil and the good" (Prov. 15:3). What a curb this would be before us if we meditated on it more often! Instead of acting recklessly, we should say with Hagar, "You are a God of seeing" (Gen. 16:13).

God's infinite knowledge should fill us with **adoration**. Our entire lives are open for Him to see from the beginning. He saw every fall, sin, and backsliding before it happened, yet, He still had His heart set on us. This realization should make us bow in wonder and worship before Him!

Reflections

God's ways are far beyond ours. What we think we know is minuscule compared to His knowledge of everything. Many theologians and scholars get wound up about how and where God gathered all this knowledge, but they miss the fact that He was and is before anything existed. All knowledge was already in Him. That includes knowing all there is to know about us, right into the deep recesses of our hearts. To think we can hide anything from Him or know something that he doesn't is to kid ourselves. It is such a mind-blowing concept that the word "omniscient" was coined to describe this elevated level of knowledge.

1. How is God's knowledge connected to His will? Why is it so important?
2. Read Psalm 139. What is your response to this very intimate knowledge God has of you?
3. Read Proverbs 1:7. Why is this the first step to gaining knowledge?
4. If God knows everything and everyone, what is the meaning of Matthew 7:23?

4

THE FOREKNOWLEDGE OF GOD

What controversies this subject has caused in the past! But what truth of the Bible has not been the center of theological battles? The deity of Christ, His virgin birth, His atoning death, His second coming; the believer's justification, sanctification, security; the church, its organization, elders, discipline; baptism, the Lord's supper, and many other precious truths can be mentioned. Yet, all the controversies did not shut the mouths of God's faithful servants, so why should we avoid the question of God's foreknowledge just because someone will accuse us of causing strife? Others can argue if they must, but our duty is to be witnesses of the light that has saved us.

Eliminating Error

There are two things concerning the foreknowledge of God that many are ignorant about: the **meaning** of the word and its **context** in the Bible. Because this ignorance is so common, it is easy for preachers and teachers to pass on their distortions even to Christians. There is only one protection against this error: to be established in the faith. For that, we need to be prayerful, diligent in studying, and humbly receptive of God's Word. Only then are we strengthened against any attacks. Some are even abusing this truth to discredit and deny the sovereignty of God in the salvation of sinners. Just as critics argue that the Bible is inspired by God and evolutionists debate His work in creation, some pseudo-Bible teachers are perverting His foreknowledge to reject His unconditional election to eternal life.

When God's foreknowledge and election of those to be conformed to the image of His Son is explained, the enemy sends along someone to argue that it is based on their interpretation of foreknowledge. Their idea of "foreknowledge" says God already knew that those who were chosen would be more flexible and respond easier to the Spirit and that because God knew they would believe, He predestined them to salvation. But such a statement is radically wrong. It rejects the truth of sin because it argues that there is something good in some people. It removes the independence of God because it makes His decrees depend on what He discovers in us. It completely turns things upside down, because in saying God foresaw certain sinners would believe in Jesus and predestined them to salvation, it is the opposite of the truth. The Bible confirms that God, in His sovereignty, singled out certain people to receive His favor (Acts 13:48), and therefore, He determined to give them the gift of faith.

False theology makes God's foreknowledge of our believing the **cause** of His election to salvation. However, God's election is the **cause**, and our believing in Jesus is the **effect** of independence.

The Truth

Let us stop for a bit and define these terms. What is meant by foreknowledge? To know something beforehand is most people's answer. But we must not jump to conclusions or turn to the dictionary as the final verdict because it is not a matter of understanding the root word. What is needed is to find out how the word is used in the Bible. The way the Holy Spirit uses an expression always defines its meaning and context. It is wrong to apply this simple rule that is responsible for so much confusion and error. So many people assume they already know the meaning of a certain word used in the Bible and do not **test** their assumptions with a concordance. Let us look at this further.

Take the word "flesh." Its meaning appears to be so obvious that many would think it is a waste of time to look up its various connections in the Bible. It is quickly assumed that the word talks about the physical body, and so no analysis is made. But, in fact, "flesh" in the Bible frequently includes far more than the physical. The meaning of the term can only be understood by comparing every time it is used and studying each separate context.

Take the word "world." The average reader of the Bible imagines this word means the human race, and consequently, many passages with this term are incorrectly interpreted.

Take the word "immortality." Surely it does not need any analysis! Obviously, it refers to the indestructibility of the soul. But it is foolish and wrong to assume anything where the Word of God is concerned. If we take the trouble to carefully examine each passage where "mortal" and "immortal" are found, we see that these words do not apply to the soul, but always to the body.

What we have said about "flesh," "world," and "immortality," also applies to "know" and "foreknow." Instead of imagining that these words mean nothing else but knowing, we must look at the different passages in which they occur to analyze each one. The word "foreknowledge" is not found in the Old Testament, but "know" is mentioned frequently. When that term is used in connection with God, it often means "to regard with favor," indicating an affection for the object, not just knowledge.

- "I **know** you by name" (Ex. 33:17).
- "You have been rebellious against the LORD from the day that I **knew** you" (Deut. 9:24).
- "Before I formed you in the womb I **knew** you" (Jer. 1:5).
- "They set up princes, but I **knew** it not" (Hos. 8:4).
- "You only have I **known** of all the families of the earth" (Amos 3:2).

In these passages "knew" means loved or appointed. In the same way, the word "know" is often used in the New Testament.

- "And then will I declare to them, 'I never **knew** you'" (Matt. 7:23).
- "I am the good shepherd. I **know** my own and my own **know** me" (John 10:14).
- "But if anyone loves God, he is **known** by God" (1 Cor. 8:3).
- "The Lord **knows** those who are his," (2 Tim. 2:19).

What Is Foreknowledge?

"Foreknowledge" as it is used in the New Testament is less ambiguous than the simple form "to know." If every passage in which it occurs is carefully studied, we discover there is no doubt it refers to the perceiving events that are yet to take place. The fact is that "foreknowledge" is never used in the Bible in connection with events or actions. Instead, it always refers to people. It is people that God "foreknows," not their actions. To prove this, we will quote each passage where it is found.

"This Jesus, delivered up according to the definite plan and foreknowledge of God, you crucified and killed" (Acts 2:23). Carefully looking at the wording of this verse, we see that the Apostle was not speaking about God's foreknowledge of the act of the crucifixion, but the person crucified.

"For those whom he foreknew he also predestined to be conformed to the image of his Son, in order that he might be the firstborn among many brothers. And those whom he predestined he also called" (Rom. 8:29-30). Look carefully at the pronoun used here. It is not **what** He foreknew, but **whom**.

It is not the surrendering of their wills nor the believing of their hearts, but surrendering themselves, that we see here. "God has not rejected his people whom he foreknew" (Rom. 11:2). Once again, we have the reference to people, nothing else.

"To those who are elect… according to the foreknowledge of God the Father" (1 Pet. 1:2). Who are the elect? They are exiles, i.e., the Diaspora, the Dispersion, and the believing Jews. Again, the reference is to people, and not to their actions.

Looking at these verses, what biblical ground is there for anyone to say God foreknew the actions of people—their repenting and believing—and because of those actions He elected them to salvation? The answer is: None! The Bible never speaks of repentance and faith as being foreseen or foreknown by God. He did know from all eternity that those chosen would repent and believe, yet this is not what the Bible refers to as the object of God's foreknowledge. The word refers to God foreknowing people. So, let us "follow the pattern of the sound words" (2 Tim. 1:13).

Another thing we must look at is that the first two verses above clearly show and teach that God's foreknowledge is not the cause, but something else lies behind and before it— His sovereign decree. Jesus was "delivered up according to [1] the definite plan and [2] foreknowledge of God" (Acts 2:23). His counsel or decree was the foundation of His foreknowledge. Romans 8:29 opens with the word *"for,"* which tells us to look at what comes before it. "All things work together for good, for those who are called according to his purpose" (Rom. 8:28). So, God's foreknowledge is based on His purpose or decree (Ps. 2:7).

God foreknows what will be because He has decreed what will be. It reverses the order of the Bible, putting the cart before the horse, to confirm that God elects because He foreknows people. The truth is, He foreknows because He has elected. This removes the cause of election from the creature and places it in God's sovereign will. God purposed to elect certain people, not because of anything good in them or from them, but out of His own pleasure. Why did He choose the ones He did? We do not know, and can only say, "Even so, Father, for so it seemed good in Your sight" (Matt. 11:26). The truth in Romans 8:29 is that before the foundation of the world, God singled out certain sinners and appointed them to salvation (2 Thess. 2:13): this is clear when it says, "predestined to be conformed to the image of his Son." God did not predestine those whom He foreknew were conformed, but those whom He foreknew (loved and elected), He predestined *"to be conformed."* Their conformity to Christ is not the cause, but the effect of God's foreknowledge and predestination.

God did not choose any sinner because He foresaw that he would believe, for the simple reason that no sinner ever believes until God gives them faith. No one sees until God gives them sight. Sight is God's gift, and seeing is the consequence of using His gift. So, faith is God's gift (Eph. 2:8,9), and believing is the consequence of using His gift. If it was true that God chose people to be saved because they would believe, then that would make believing a worthy action, and the saved sinner would be able to boast about it, which the Bible denies (Eph. 2:9).

God's Word is clear enough to teach us that believing is not a worthy action. It says that Christians are people who "through grace had believed" (Acts 18:27). If, we have believed *"through grace,"* there is nothing admirable about believing—it could not be reason that caused God to choose us. God's choice does not come from anything in or from us, but purely from His sovereign pleasure. In Romans 11:5, we read about "a remnant, chosen by grace." That is clear! Election is of grace, and grace is undeserved favor, something which we had no claim on God at all.

So, it is important for us to have clear, spiritual views of the foreknowledge of God. Inaccurate ideas about it always end in thoughts that dishonor Him. The popular idea of divine foreknowledge is completely inadequate. God not only knew the end from the beginning, but He planned, fixed, and predestined everything from the beginning. And, as cause stands to effect, so God's purpose is the basis of His foresight. If you are a true Christian, it is because God chose you in Christ before the foundation of the world (Eph. 1:4). He did not choose because He foresaw you would believe, but simply because it pleased Him to choose you, despite your natural unbelief. So, all the glory and praise is His, and no one else's. You have no reason for taking any credit for yourself. You have believed *"through grace,"* because your election was *"by grace."*

Reflections

The future can be intriguing and scary at the same time, venturing into the unknown. But with God, nothing is unknown or uncertain. He does not just see ahead, he has known and predestined what will be before time began, before eternity. Our finite minds struggle to comprehend that. It also flies in the face of our understanding of free will and choice. It's almost easier to just throw up our hands and let "fate" take its toll if that's the case! As Pink says, this attribute alone can be a real stumbling block for Christians. But God is not a watchmaker who has wound the clock and stepped back to simply let it all wind down—He is involved! That makes the difference. There is a relationship in all of this, and He has called us into it with Him.

1. What is your understanding of foreknowledge?
2. Is God's foreknowledge a comfort or a frustration for you?
3. How do you explain a verse like Psalm 139:4?
4. Ephesians 1:4-5 says, *"In love He predestined..."* What role does love play in God's foreknowledge?
5. If God has predestined things for you, what do you think your reaction or response be?

5

THE SUPREMACY OF GOD

Many Do Not Know Him

In one of his letters to Erasmus, Luther said, "Your thoughts of God are too human" (2010/1525, 12.XVI). That renowned scholar probably resented the rebuke since it came from a miner's son; however, it was thoroughly deserved. We would not mind the same accusation being brought against most of today's preachers who lazily accept the teaching of others instead of searching the Bible for themselves. The most dishonoring and degrading theories of the rule and reign of God are now taught and believed everywhere. To thousands, even those who call themselves Christians, the God of the Bible is virtually unknown.

God complained to backslidden Israel, "You thought that I was one like yourself" (Ps. 50:21). This same accusation is brought against backslidden Christianity. People imagine that the Most High is moved by emotion, rather than principle. They think His omnipotence is just fiction and that Satan is blocking His designs on every side. They think that if He has formed any plan or purpose, then it must be like theirs, constantly subject to change. They say that whatever power He has is restricted, otherwise He would invade the strength of people's free will and reduce them to nothing but robots. They dilute the powerful atonement of redemption to nothing more than a remedy, which sin-sick souls can use if they want it. They undermine the invincible work of the Holy Spirit to an offer that sinners can accept or reject.

The "god" of this modern age does not resemble the Supreme Sovereign of the Bible any more than the dim flickering of a candle can show the glory of the midday sun. The "god" who is preached from average pulpits, spoken about in ordinary Sunday Schools, mentioned in most religious books, and preached in most so-called Bible conferences is the figment of human imagination, an invention of emotional sentimentality. The non-believer makes gods out of wood and stone, while millions of "believers" manufacture a "god" out of their natural minds. They are actually atheists because there is no other alternative between an absolutely supreme God and no God at all. A "god" whose will is resisted, whose designs are frustrated, whose purpose is checkmated, cannot be God and does not deserve worship, only disapproval.

King of Kings and Lord of Lords

The supremacy of the true and living God is often viewed regarding the huge distance separating the mightiest creatures from the almighty Creator. He is the Potter, we are just clay in His hands, to be molded into vessels of honor or to be dashed into pieces as He pleases (Ps. 2:9). If all the citizens of heaven and earth joined in revolt against Him, it would not affect Him, having less effect on His eternal throne than the spray of the Mediterranean's waves on the rocks of Gibraltar—trivial and powerless. The Bible tells us that when the Gentiles unite with backslidden Israel to defy Jehovah, "He who sits in the heavens laughs" (Ps. 2:4).

The absolute and universal supremacy of God is clearly confirmed in many verses:

- "Yours, O LORD, is the greatness and the power and the glory and the victory and the majesty, for all that is in the heavens and in the earth is yours. Yours is the kingdom, O Lord, and you are exalted as head above all… and you rule over all" (1 Chron. 29:11,12). It says, *"rule"* now, not will rule in the future.
- "O LORD, God of our fathers, are you not God in heaven? You rule over all the kingdoms of the nations. In your hand are power and might, so that none is able to withstand you" (2 Chron. 20:6). Before Him presidents and popes, kings and emperors, are less than grasshoppers.
- "But he is unchangeable, and who can turn him back? What he desires, that he does" (Job 23:13). The God of the Bible is no make-believe monarch, no imaginary sovereign, but King of kings, and Lord of lords.

- "I know that you can do all things, and that no purpose of yours can be thwarted" (Job 42:2). No thought hindered; no purpose frustrated. All He has designed, He does. All He has decreed, He performs.
- "Our God is in the heavens; he does all that he pleases" (Ps. 115:3)
- Why? Because "no wisdom, no understanding, no counsel can avail against the LORD" (Prov. 21:30).

Whatever Pleased the Lord

God's supremacy over the works of His hands is clearly shown in the Bible. Lifeless matter, irrational creatures, all obey their Maker's orders.

- He parted the Red Sea and the water stood up as walls (Ex. 14).
- The earth opened its mouth, and the guilty fell into the pit (Num. 16).
- When He ordered, the sun stood still (Josh. 10).
- The sun even reversed ten degrees on the dial of Ahaz (Isa. 38:8).
- To show His supremacy, He made ravens carry food to Elijah (I Kings 17).
- He made iron float on water (2 Kings 6:5).
- He caused lions to be tame when Daniel was thrown into the den and stopped the fire from burning the three Hebrews when they were thrown into the flames.

"Whatever the Lord pleases, he does, in heaven and on earth, in the seas and all deeps" (Ps. 135:6). God's supremacy is also demonstrated in His perfect rule over people's wills. Look at Exodus 34:24. Three times a year, all the men of Israel had to leave their homes and go to Jerusalem. They lived among hostile people, who hated them for having taken their lands. So, what stopped the Canaanites from seizing the opportunity when the Israelite men were gone, killing the women and children, and taking their farms? If the Almighty hand was not on the wills of wicked men, how could He promise that no one would even desire their lands? "The king's heart is a stream of water in the hand of the LORD; he turns it wherever he will" (Prov. 21:1).

But do we not read in the Bible how people defied God, resisted His will, broke His commandments, disregarded His warnings, and turned a deaf ear to all His words? We do. Does this undermine everything we have already said? If it does, then the Bible contradicts itself. But that cannot be. What the argument refers to is the wickedness of man against the external Word of God, whereas what we have mentioned before is what God has **purposed in Himself.** The way He has given us to walk in is not perfectly fulfilled by us, only by His own eternal counsel are they achieved to the smallest details.

The absolute and universal supremacy of God is also clearly confirmed in the New Testament. We are told that God "works all things according to the counsel of his will" (Eph. 1:11). The Greek for *"works"* means "to work effectively."

That is why we read, "For from him and through him and to him are all things. To him be glory forever. Amen" (Rom. 11:36). People can boast that they are free agents, with a will of their own, and free to do as they please, but the Bible says to them, "You who say, 'Today or tomorrow we will go into such and such a town and spend a year there and trade and make a profit… Instead, you ought to say, "If the Lord wills, we will live and do this or that" (James 4:13-15)!

The heart can find peace in this. Our lives are not the product of blind fate and not the result of chance, but every detail was ordained from all eternity and is now ordered by the living and reigning God. Not a hair of our heads can be touched without His permission.

"The heart of man plans his way, but the Lord establishes his steps" (Prov. 16:9).

What assurance, strength, and comfort this should give us as Christians!

"My times are in your hand" (Ps. 31:15).

Then let me "be still before the LORD and wait patiently for him" (Ps. 37:7).

Reflections

There is a definite hierarchy that exists in the spiritual and physical realms. Certain angels have tasks and status that elevate them, as there are people who hold higher ranks above others. But to think God fits anywhere in this, would be foolish and small-minded. He is completely above all and everything. There is no level that comes close to Him. Not only that; He is independent of everything and everyone. He has no need of angels, people, and planets. They are all there for His own pleasure and purpose. This is the meaning of supreme—where He exists above and beyond. To try and bring Him down to our level or even that of other entities is blasphemy.

1. Why do you think people always try to bring God down to their level?
2. What is the spiritual outcome of doing this?
3. Read John 3:31. What is your explanation for this verse?
4. What should our response be when it comes to acknowledging God's supremacy?

6

THE SOVEREIGNTY OF GOD

What Is It?

The sovereignty of God can be defined as His supremacy being exercised or implemented.

Being lifted far above the highest creature, He is the Most High, Lord of heaven and earth, subject to no one, influenced by no one, completely independent. God does as He pleases, only as He pleases, always as He pleases. No one can stop or distract Him. His own Word says:

- "My counsel shall stand, and I will accomplish all my purpose" (Isa. 46:10).
- "He does according to his will among the host of heaven and among the inhabitants of the earth; and none can stay his hand" (Dan. 4:35).

God's sovereignty means that He is God in name and fact—He is on the Throne of the universe, directing all things, working all things "according to the counsel of his will" (Eph. 1:11).

In his sermon on Matthew 20:15, Charles Spurgeon (2024a) said:

There is no attribute more comforting to His children than God's sovereignty. Under the most adverse circumstances, in the most severe trials, they believe that sovereignty has ordained their afflictions, that sovereignty overrules them, and that sovereignty will sanctify them all. There is nothing the children should contend with other than the doctrine of their Master over all creation—the kingship of God over all the works of His own hands—the throne of God and His right to sit upon that throne. On the other hand, there is no doctrine more hated by the world, no truth which they have made such a [toy], as the great, stupendous, yet most certain doctrine of the sovereignty of the infinite Jehovah. Men will allow God to be everywhere except on His throne. They will allow Him to be in His workshop to fashion worlds and make stars. They will allow Him to be in His storehouse to dispense His bounties. They will allow Him to sustain the earth and hold up its pillars, or light the lamps of heaven, or rule the waves of the ever-moving ocean; but when God ascends His throne, His creatures gnash their teeth. And we proclaim an enthroned God, and His right to do as He wills with His own, to dispose of His creatures as He thinks, without consulting them in the matter; then we are hissed and hated, and then men turn a deaf ear to us, for God on His throne is not the God they love. But it is God on the throne that we love to preach. It is God on His throne whom we trust.

"Whatever the Lord pleases, he does, in heaven and on earth, in the seas and all deeps" (Ps. 135:6). This is the majestic ruler we see in the Bible. Unrivaled in majesty, unlimited in power, unaffected by anything outside Himself. But we are living in a day when even the most orthodox are afraid to admit the proper Godhood of God. They say that the sovereignty of God excludes human responsibility; even though human responsibility is based on divine sovereignty and is the product of it.

Our Responsibility and His Sovereignty

"Our God is in the heavens; he does all that he pleases" (Ps. 115:3). He sovereignly chose to place His creatures in positions that seemed good in His sight. He created angels: some He gave a conditional status, others He allowed to stand before Him (1 Tim. 5:21), making Jesus their head (Col. 2:10). The angels that sinned were as much His creatures as the angels that did not sin (2 Pet. 2:4). Yet God foresaw they would fall, and still placed them on a conditional status, and allowed them to fall, even though He was not the Author of their sin.

In the same way, God sovereignly placed Adam in the Garden of Eden on a conditional footing. He could have given him an unconditional status if He wanted. He could have placed him on the same steady position as the unfallen angels. He could have placed him on the same established place that His saints have in Jesus. But, instead, He chose to set him in

Eden so that he stood or fell according to his responsibility—obedience to his Maker. Adam was accountable to God by the law that his Creator had given him. This was responsibility, unimpaired responsibility, tested under the most favorable conditions.

Now God did not place Adam there because He had to. No, it was right because God did it. God did not give creatures life because it was right for Him to do so—because He was under any obligation to create—but it was right because He did so. God is sovereign. His will is supreme. God is not under any law of right; He is a law unto Himself so that whatsoever He does is right.

To anyone who questions His sovereignty, He says, "Woe to him who strives with him who formed him, a pot among earthen pots! Does the clay say to him who forms it, 'What are you making?' or 'Your work has no handles'?" (Isa.45:9).

God sovereignly placed Israel on a conditional standing. Exodus 19, 20, and 24 give us clear proof of this. They were placed under a covenant of works. God gave them certain laws, and they were blessed depending on whether they observed these or not. But Israel was stiff-necked and uncircumcised in heart. They rebelled against Jehovah, ignored His law, turned to false gods, and turned away. The consequence was that divine judgment fell on them, and they were delivered into the hands of their enemies, dispersed throughout the earth, and remain under God's displeasure to this day.

It was God exercising His high sovereignty that put Satan and his angels, Adam, and Israel in their respective positions.

His sovereignty did not take away responsibility from the creature, but in exercising it, He gave them this conditional status with responsibilities He thought were suitable for each. By this sovereignty, He is seen as God overall. So, there is perfect harmony between the sovereignty of God and the responsibility of the creature. Many have foolishly said that it is impossible to show where God's sovereignty ends and a created being's accountability begins. The creature's responsibility begins in the sovereign anointing of the Creator. There is no end to His sovereignty and there never will be any!

Let us look at more proof that the created being's responsibility is based on God's sovereignty. How many things in the Bible were right because God commanded them and would not have been right if He had not commanded them? What right did Adam have to eat of the trees of the Garden? He had the permission of his Maker, without which he would have been a thief (Gen. 2:16)! What right did Israel have to borrow the Egyptians' jewels (Ex. 12:35)? None, unless Jehovah had authorized it (Exo 3:22). What right did Israel have to kill so many lambs for sacrifice? None, except that God commanded it. What right did Israel have to kill all the Canaanites? None, except that Jehovah commanded them. What right does the husband have to require submission from his wife? None, unless God appointed it.

So, we can go on. Human responsibility is based on divine sovereignty.

One more example of God exercising His absolute sovereignty is when He put His chosen people on a different status from Adam or Israel. He placed His elect on an **un**conditional standing. In the New Covenant, Jesus was appointed as their head, took their responsibilities on Himself, and produced a righteousness for them that is perfect and eternal. Jesus was placed on a conditional standing, because He was "born under the law, to redeem those who were under the law" (Gal. 4:4-5), with only one difference—the others failed. He did not and could not. And who put Jesus Christ in that conditional position? The Triune God. It was sovereign will that appointed Him, sovereign love that sent Him, and sovereign authority that assigned Him His work.

Certain conditions were given to the Mediator. He was to be made in the image of sinful flesh. He was to magnify the law and make it honorable. He was to bear the sins of God's people in His body on the cross. He was to make full atonement for them. He was to endure the judgment of God. He was to die and be buried. Once those conditions were fulfilled, He was promised a reward (Isa. 53:10-12). He was to be the Firstborn among many. He was to have a people who would share His glory. Blessed be His name forever, He fulfilled those conditions, and because He did, the Father is sworn to preserve and bless all those for whom Jesus mediated. Because He took their place, they now share His. His righteousness is theirs, His position before God is theirs, and His life is theirs. There is not a single condition for them to meet, not a single responsibility for them to fulfill to achieve eternal happiness. "For by a single offering he has perfected for all time those who are being sanctified [set apart]" (Heb. 10:14).

This is the sovereignty of God displayed in different ways for everyone, in the ways He has dealt with His creatures. Some of the angels, Adam, and Israel were placed on a conditional footing, their blessing dependent on their obedience and loyalty to God. But in sharp contrast, the "little flock" (Luke 12:32) has been given an unconditional, immutable position in God's covenant, counsel, and Son. Their blessing is dependent on what Jesus did for them. "God's firm foundation stands, bearing this seal: 'The Lord knows those who are his'" (2 Tim. 2:19). The foundation on which God's chosen stand is perfect: nothing can be added or taken from it (Eccl. 3:14). This is the highest and most wonderful display of the absolute sovereignty of God. "He has mercy on whomever he wills, and he hardens whomever he wills" (Rom. 9:18).

Reflections

The term sovereign has been lost on us in this modern age where there are very few monarchs and hardly any of those have absolute power. To understand God's dominion and rule is to see Him as in total control over everything and everyone —even Satan! He has the wisdom, power, and authority to do whatever He chooses to do. Too many Christians have become facetious and flippant in their friendship with God. They treat Him more as a buddy or a jackpot machine than an all-powerful deity whose ways are always far higher than ours. To realize His sovereignty is to bring us to a reverent appreciation and awe for the King of kings and Lord of lords.

1. Do you like being in charge or not in charge?

2. Do you ever struggle to allow God to be in charge of your life? Why?
3. Read John 10:17-18. What does this say about God's sovereignty?
4. How will accepting God as sovereign affect your prayer and worship life?

7

THE IMMUTABILITY OF GOD

Different From His Creation

Immutability is one of God's attributes that is not given enough thought. It is one of the Creator's characteristics that distinguish Him from all His creatures. God is always the same—never changing in His being, attributes, or determinations. God is compared to a "rock" that cannot be moved when the entire ocean surrounding it is in constant fluctuation (Deut. 32:4). Even though all creatures are subject to change, God is immutable and permanent. Because God has no beginning and no end, He knows no change. He is the eternal "Father of lights, with whom there is no variation or shadow due to change" (James 1:17).

Aspects of His immutability

1. Immutable in His **essence**. His nature and being are infinite, not subject to change. There was never a time when He was not; there will never come a time when He will stop being God. He has not evolved, grown, or improved. Everything He is today, He has always been and will always be. He confirms this by saying, "I the LORD do not change" (Mal. 3:6). He cannot change for the better, because He is already perfect. Being perfect, He cannot change for the worse. Because He is unaffected by anything outside Himself, improvement or deterioration is impossible. He is always the same. Only He can say, "I AM WHO I AM" (Ex. 3:14). He is not influenced by time. There is no wrinkle on the brow of eternity. Therefore, His power cannot diminish, and His glory cannot fade.
2. Immutable in His **attributes**. Whatever attributes God had before the universe was called into existence, they are the same now and will remain like that forever. They are the perfections and essential qualities of His being. *Semper idem* (always the same) is written on each of them. His power is unrestricted, His wisdom undiminished, His holiness faultless. The attributes of God cannot change any more than He can stop from being God. His truth is immutable and permanent because His Word is "forever... fixed in the heavens" (Ps. 119:89). His love is eternal: "I have loved you with an everlasting love" (Jer. 31:3) and "having loved his own who were in the world, he

loved them to the end" (John 13:1). His mercy never ceases, because it is "everlasting" (Ps. 100:5).
3. Immutable in His **counsel**. His will never changes. Some people might try to argue this because of the verse: "And the LORD regretted that he had made man on the earth" (Gen. 6:6). Does the Bible contradict itself? No, that cannot be. Numbers 23:19 is clear: "God is not man, that he should lie, or a son of man, that he should change his mind." In 1 Samuel 15:29, "The Glory of Israel will not lie or have regret, for he is not a man, that he should have regret." The explanation is simple. When speaking of Himself, God often uses language that our limited minds can understand. He describes Himself as having body parts: eyes, ears, hands, and so on. He speaks about waking up and "rising up early" (Jer. 7:13), and yet, He does not sleep. When He makes a change in the way He deals with people, He describes it as regret. Yes, God is immutable in His counsel. "For the gifts and the calling of God are irrevocable" (Rom. 11:29). It must be so, for "He is unique, and who can make Him change? And whatever His soul desires, that He does" (Job 23:13).

Though change and decay are in all around we see, may He who never changes abide with thee.

God's purpose never changes. One of two things causes a man to change his mind and reverse his plans: not having enough foresight to anticipate everything or lack of power to execute them. But since God is both omniscient and omnipotent, there is no need for Him to revise His decrees. "The counsel of the LORD stands forever, the plans of his heart to all generations" (Ps. 33:11). That is why it mentions "the unchangeable character of his purpose" (Heb. 6:17).

Are We Dependable?

Now we can see the infinite distance that separates the highest creature from the Creator. A created being and mutability are terms that go together. If the creature was not mutable by nature, it would not be a creature—it would be God. By nature, we lean toward nothingness, since we came from nothing. We are kept from extinction only by the will and sustaining power of God. No one can sustain themselves for a single moment. We are completely dependent on the Creator for every breath we take. We can only say that God "has kept our soul among the living" (Ps. 66:9). The realization of this should cause us to bow low because of our nothingness in the presence of Him in whom "we live and move and have our being" (Acts 17:28).

As fallen creatures, we are not just mutable, but everything in us is opposed to God. We are "wandering stars" (Jude 13), out of our proper orbit. "The wicked are like the tossing sea; for it cannot be quiet" (Isa. 57:20). Fallen man is inconstant. The words of Jacob about Reuben apply to all of Adam's descendants: "unstable as water" (Gen. 49:4). So, it is not only a sign of godliness, but also wisdom to observe the warning to "stop regarding man" (Isa. 2:22). No human being can be depended on. "Put not your trust in princes, in a son of man, in whom there is no salvation" (Ps. 146:3). If I disobey God, then I deserve to be deceived and disappointed by people. Those who like you today may hate you tomorrow. The crowds that shouted, "Hosanna to the Son of David," quickly changed to "Away with Him, crucify Him."

Being Established

1. It is a **solid comfort**. We cannot rely on human nature, but we can rely on God! However unstable I might be, however fickle my friends prove to be, God does not change. If He changed as we do, if He wanted one thing today and another tomorrow, if He was controlled by impulse, who could confide in Him? But, praise to His glorious name, He is always the same. His purpose is fixed, His will is stable, and His word is sure. This is a rock on which we can establish our feet while the storm is sweeping away everything around us. The permanence of God's character guarantees the fulfillment of His promises: "For the mountains may depart and the hills be removed, but my steadfast love shall not depart from you, and my covenant of peace shall not be removed," says the Lord, who has compassion on you" (Isa. 54:10).
2. It is an **encouragement to pray**. What comfort would it be to pray to a god that, like the chameleon, changed color every moment? Who would put up a petition to an earthly prince that was so mutable as to grant a petition one day, and deny it another? (Stephen Charnock, 1670). What if someone asks,

"What is the use of praying to a god whose will is already fixed?" The answer is that He requires it. What blessings has God promised without us seeking them? "If we ask anything according to his will he hears us," and He has willed everything that is for His child's good (1 John 5:14). To ask for anything contrary to His will is not prayer, but rebellion.

3. It is a **fear for the wicked**. Those who defy Him, who break His laws, who have no concern for His glory, but who live their lives as though He did not exist, must not think that when they cry to Him for mercy on that last day, He will change His will, cancel His word, and withdraw His judgment. No, He has declared, "Therefore I will act in wrath. My eye will not spare, nor will I have pity. And though they cry in my ears with a loud voice, I will not hear them" (Ez. 8:18). God will not deny Himself to satisfy their lusts. God is holy and does not change. Therefore, God hates sin and eternally hates it. That is why the punishment of all who die in their sins is an eternal one. John Dick (2021) explained it like this:

The divine immutability, like the cloud that intervened between the Israelites and the Egyptian army, has a dark as well as a light side. It ensures the execution of His threats, as well as the performance of His promises; and destroys the hope that the guilty fondly cherish, that He will be lenient to His frail and erring creatures, and that they will be dealt with more lightly than the declarations of His own Word would lead us to expect. We oppose these deceitful and presumptuous speculations of the solemn truth, that God is unchanging in veracity and purpose, in faithfulness and justice.

Reflections

Immutability is not a word we often use in modern-day meetings or chats, just like omniscience and omnipotence. But sometimes there is no other way to express a complex concept except with a wonderful, big word. Basically, immutability means something that does not change and is fitting for God because He is permanent in all His ways and character. For us as humans, this can be a foreign idea since we live in a world that is always changing and we deal with emotions that are up one day and down the next. But it can be an incredible rock for us, knowing that despite the turmoil and shifting landscapes, God remains!

1. Which picture of God's immutability appeals to you most? An anchor or a rock?
2. Do you ever think of God's unchangeable character and what it means for you?
3. What effect does this attribute have on God's promises and plans?
4. What does Hebrews 13:8 mean for you?

8

THE HOLINESS OF GOD

Only He Is Holy

"Who will not fear, O Lord, and glorify your name? For you alone are holy" (Rev. 15:4). Only He is independently, infinitely, immutably holy. The Bible often calls Him the Holy One, because all moral goodness is in Him. He is completely pure, untouched by the smallest trace of sin. "God is light, and in him is no darkness at all" (1 John 1:5). Holiness is the very excellency of the divine nature: the great God is *"majestic in holiness"* (Exo. 15:11). So, we read, "You who are of purer eyes than to see evil and cannot look at wrong" (Hab. 1:13). God's power is the opposite of our natural weakness, His wisdom is in contrast to the smallest flaw of our understanding or foolishness, and His holiness is the antithesis of all moral imperfection.

In the Old Testament, God appointed singers in Israel "who should raise the beauty of holiness" (2 Chron. 20:21). "Power is God's hand or arm, omniscience His eye, mercy His bowels, eternity His duration, but holiness is His beauty" (Charnock, 2023). This is what makes Him beautiful to those who are delivered from sin's captivity.

God's perfection is emphasized:

God is called Holy more often than Almighty and set apart by His dignity more than by any other. This is more fixed to His name than any other. You never find it expressed "His mighty name" or "His wise name," but His great name, and most of all, His holy name. This is the greatest title of honor, and in this, the majesty of His name appears. (Charnock)

This perfection is celebrated before the Throne of Heaven, as the angels cry, "Holy, holy, holy is the LORD of hosts" (Isa. 6:3). God Himself highlights this perfection, "Once for all I have sworn by my holiness" (Ps. 89:35). He swears by His *"holiness"* because is the best expression of Himself than anything else. So, we are encouraged to "sing praises to the LORD, O you his saints, and give thanks to his holy name" (Ps. 30:4). "This may be said to be a [supernatural] attribute, that runs through the rest, and casts a glow on them. It is an attribute of attributes" (Howe, 1822). So, we read: "the beauty of the LORD" (Ps. 27:4), which is none other than "the beauties of holiness" (Ps. 110:3).

As it seems to challenge all His other perfections, so it is the glory of all the rest: as it is the glory of the Godhead, so it is the glory of every perfection in the Godhead; as His power is the strength of them, so His holiness is the beauty of them; as all would be weak without strength to back them, so all would be ugly without holiness to adorn them. Should this be destroyed, all the rest would lose their honor; just as if the sun should lose its light, it would also lose its heat, its strength, its energy. As sincerity is the glow of every grace in a Christian, so purity is the splendor of every attribute in the Godhead. His justice is a holy justice, His wisdom a holy wisdom, His power a "holy arm" (Ps. 98:1). His truth or promise is a "holy promise" (Ps. 105:42). His name, which signifies all His attributes in conjunction is "holy" (Ps. 103:1).

His Holiness Revealed

- God's holiness is revealed **in His works.** "The LORD is righteous in all his ways, and holy in all his works" (Ps. 145:17). Only excellence can come from Him. Holiness is the rule of all His actions. In the beginning, He said that all He made was "very good" (Gen. 1:31). He could not have done that if there was anything imperfect or unholy in them. Man was made "upright" in the image and likeness of his Creator (Eccl. 7:29). The angels that fell were created holy because we are told that they "did not stay within their own position… their proper dwelling" (Jude 6). And the Bible says about Satan: "You were blameless in your ways from the day you were created, till unrighteousness was found in you" (Eze. 28:15).

- God's holiness is revealed **in His law**. That law forbids sin in all its ways: in its most polished and worst forms, the thoughts and the impure actions, the secret desire as well as the public deeds. So, we read, "The law is holy, and the commandment is holy and righteous and good" (Rom. 7:12). Yes, "The precepts of the Lord are right, rejoicing the heart; the commandment of the Lord is pure, enlightening the eyes" (Ps. 19:8,9).
- God's holiness is revealed **at the cross**. The atonement displays God's infinite holiness and hatred of sin. How terrible sin must be to God for Him to punish it to the full degree when it was imputed to His Son!

Not all the vials of judgment that have or shall be poured out upon the wicked world, nor the flaming furnace of a sinner's conscience, nor the irreversible sentence pronounced against the rebellious demons, nor the groans of the damned creatures, give such a demonstration of God's hatred of sin, as the wrath of God let loose upon His Son. Never did divine holiness appear more beautiful and lovely than at the time our Savior's countenance was most marred in the midst of His dying groans. He acknowledges this in Psalm 22. When God had turned His smiling face from Him, and thrust His sharp knife into His heart, which forced that terrible cry from Him, "My God, My God, why hast Thou forsaken Me?" He adores this perfection—"You are holy" (v.3) (Charnock).

- Because God is holy, He **hates all sin**. He loves everything that conforms to His laws and hates everything contrary to it. The Bible says, "The devious person is an abomination to the LORD" (Prov. 3:32). And again, "The thoughts of the wicked are an abomination to the LORD" (Prov. 15:26). So, He must punish sin. Sin cannot exist without His punishment and His hatred of it. God has often forgiven sinners, but He never forgives sin, and the sinner is only forgiven when someone else takes on their punishment: "Without the shedding of blood there is no forgiveness" (Heb. 9:22). So, we are told "The Lord takes vengeance on his adversaries and keeps wrath for his enemies" (Nah. 1:2). For one sin, God exiled Adam and Eve from Eden. For one sin, all of Canaan fell under a curse that remains to this day (Gen. 9:21). For one sin, Moses was excluded from the Promised Land, Elisha's servant was struck with leprosy, and Ananias and Sapphira were killed.

A World View of His Holiness

This is proof of the divine inspiration of the Bible. Non-believers do not believe in the holiness of God. Their idea of His character is completely one-sided. They hope that His mercy will cover everything else. "You thought that I was one like yourself" is God's accusation against them (Ps. 50:21). They think only of a god after their own evil hearts. So, they continue in their foolishness. The holiness given to God's nature and character in the Bible clearly demonstrates their supernatural origin. The character attributed to the ancient heathen gods is the reverse of that immaculate purity pertaining to the true God. A holy God who hates all sin was never invented by any of Adam's fallen descendants! The fact is that nothing reveals the depravity of man's heart and his hostility to the living God than to have One who is infinitely and immutably holy set before him. His own idea of sin is limited to what the world calls crime. Anything else, people describe as defects, mistakes, and weaknesses. And even when they own up to sin, they make excuses and justifications for it. The god that most Christians 'love' is seen as an indulgent old man who does not like foolishness but leniently winks at the indiscretions of youth.

But the Bible says, "You hate all evildoers" (Ps. 5:5). And again, "God is angry with the wicked every day" (Ps. 7:11 NKJV). But people refuse to believe in this God, and they gnash their teeth when His hatred of sin is faithfully brought to their attention. No sinful person will invent a holy God any more than they will create a Lake of Fire that will torment them forever.

Because God is holy, accepting Him on a natural level is completely impossible. A fallen person would be more likely to create a world than produce something that would meet the approval of God's purity. Can darkness live with Light? Can the spotless One take pleasure in "a polluted garment" (Isa. 64:6)? The best that sinful people produce is contaminated. A corrupt tree cannot bear good fruit. God would deny Himself and downgrade His perfections if He accepted unrighteousness and unholiness as righteous and holy. Everything that has the smallest stain on it is contrary to the nature of God.

What His holiness demanded, His grace provided in Jesus. Every sinner who has fled to Him for refuge stands "blessed… in the Beloved" (Eph. 1:6). Hallelujah!

When We Come to God

- Because God is holy, the **highest reverence** is necessary when we come to Him. "God greatly to be feared in the council of the holy ones, and awesome above all who are around him" (Ps. 89:7). "Exalt the Lord our God; worship at his footstool! Holy is he" (Ps. 99:5). Yes, *"at his footstool,"* in the lowest posture of humility, bowing low before Him. When Moses came to the burning bush, God said, "Take your sandals off your feet" (Exo 3:5). He is to be served "with fear" (Ps. 2:11). His demand of Israel was, "I will be sanctified, and before all the people I will be glorified" (Lev. 10:3). The more our hearts are in awe of His holiness, the more acceptable our approach to Him will be.
- Because God is holy, we should want to be **conformed to Him**. His commandment is, "You shall be holy, for I am holy" (1 Pet. 1:16). We are not told to be omnipotent or omniscient as God is, but we are to be holy "in all your conduct" (1 Pet. 1:15).

This is the prime way of honoring God. We do not glorify God by elevated admirations, or eloquent expressions, or pompous services for Him as when we aspire to conversing with Him with unstained spirits, and live for Him in living like Him (Charnock, 1840).

God alone is the source of holiness, so let us seek holiness from Him. Let our daily prayer be that He may "sanctify you completely, and may your whole spirit and soul and body be kept blameless at the coming of our Lord Jesus Christ" (1 Thess. 5:23).

Reflections

Holiness is not an easy concept for us because our limited understanding is of something good. We sometimes call a religious or pious person holy because they lead such a moral life. But with God, He goes beyond just good and moral—He is perfectly devoid of anything bad, any sin, and any corruption. Our best goodness comes nowhere near His holiness. It goes far beyond any human condition. When we comprehend just what this means, we will also be compelled to bow down and cry, "Holy, holy, holy!"

1. What is your definition of holiness?
2. Can you think of a person in your life (other than Jesus) who might be called holy?
3. Do you think Christians give enough reverence and holy fear to God's holiness in church these days?
4. What do you think of the words in Leviticus 19:2? Read 1 Peter 1:16.
5. Do you think it is possible to be holy? Why and how?

9

THE POWER OF GOD

The Right Concept of His Power

We cannot have the right idea of God unless we think of Him as all-powerful, not just all-wise. Anyone who cannot do what he wants as he pleases cannot be God. As much as God has a will to decide what is good, so He has power to carry it out.

The power of God is the ability and strength that He can bring to pass whatever He pleases, whatever His infinite wisdom may direct, and whatever the infinite purity of His will may resolve. As holiness is the beauty of all God's attributes, so power gives life and action to all the perfections of the divine nature. How vain would the eternal counsel be, if power did not step in to carry them out? Without power His mercy would just be feeble pity, His promises an empty sound, and His threats a scarecrow. God's power is like

Himself: infinite, eternal, incomprehensible; it cannot be checked, restrained, nor frustrated by the creature.

"Once God has spoken; twice have I heard this: that power belongs to God" (Ps. 62:11).

- *"Once God has spoken."* Nothing else is necessary!

Heaven and earth will pass away, but His word abides forever. *"Once God has spoken"*: how fitting for His majesty! Poor mortals like us might speak often and yet fail to be heard. He speaks only once, and the thunder of His power is heard on a thousand hills.

The Lord also thundered in the heavens, and the Most High uttered his voice,

hailstones and coals of fire. And he sent out his arrows and scattered them;

he flashed forth lightnings and routed them.

Then the channels of the sea were seen,

and the foundations of the world were laid bare at your rebuke,

O Lord, at the blast of the breath of your nostrils. (Ps. 18:13-15)

- *"Once God has spoken."* See His unchanging authority. "For who in the skies can be compared to the Lord? Who among the heavenly beings[a] is like the Lord" (Ps. 89:6).

All the inhabitants of the earth are accounted as nothing, and he does according to his will among the host of heaven and among the inhabitants of the earth; and none can stay his hand or say to him, 'What have you done?'" (Dan. 4:35)

This was clearly displayed when God became incarnate and lived among people. To the leper, He said, "'I will; be clean.' And immediately his leprosy was cleansed" (Matt. 8:3). To the one who was in the grave for four days He cried, "Lazarus, come out," and the dead man came out. The wind and the angry waves were silenced by a single word from Him. A legion of demons could not resist His authoritative command.

His Power, Our Pride

"Power belongs to God," and to Him alone. No being in the entire universe has an atom of power except what God gives it. But God's power is not acquired, nor does it depend on any recognition by any other authority. It belongs to Him inherently. God's power is like Himself: self-existent, self-sustained. The strongest person cannot add any power to the Omnipotent One. He does not sit on a reinforced throne or lean on supporting arms. His court is not maintained by servants and does not borrow splendor from His creatures. He is the central source and originator of all power.

Not only does all creation bear witness to the great power of God, but also His independence from all created things. Listen to His own challenge:

Where were you when I laid the foundation of the earth? Tell me, if you have understanding. Who determined its measurements—surely you know! Or who stretched the line upon it? On what were its bases sunk, or who laid its cornerstone? (Job 38:4-6)

The pride of humans is completely thrown in the dust!

Power is also used as a name of God. "Son of Man seated at the right hand of Power" (Mark 14:62), the right hand of God. God and power are so inseparable that they are combined. He is so immense, not confined in place; He is eternal, not measured in time; He is almighty, not limited in action.

When He Hides His Power

"Behold, these are but the outskirts of his ways, and how small a whisper do we hear of him! But the thunder of his power who can understand?" (Job 26:14). Who is able to count all the monuments of His power? His power we see in creation is beyond our understanding, so His omnipotence is even further from being comprehended. There is infinitely more power in the nature of God than in all His works.

"Outskirts of his ways." Only parts of it we see in creation, providence, and redemption. "And there he veiled his power" (Hab. 3:4). It is hardly possible to imagine anything more incredible than the picture of this whole chapter, yet nothing in it surpasses the nobility of this verse. The prophet saw the mighty God scattering the hills and overturning the mountains, which should have been an amazing demonstration of

His power. But this verse says He demonstrates it in hiding his power instead of displaying it. What does this mean? The power of God is so inconceivable, so immense, so uncontrollable, that the tremors He works in nature hide more than they reveal of His infinite might!

The Magnitude of His Power

It is beautiful to link the following verses together: He "trampled the waves of the sea" (Job 9:8), which expresses God's uncontrollable power. "He walks on the vault of heaven" (Job 22:14), which tells of the immensity of His presence. He "rides on the wings of the wind" (Ps. 104:3), which signifies the amazing speed of His operations. This last expression is remarkable. He does not fly, run, or walk on the wings of the wind. One of the most reckless elements, tossed into a rage and sweeping along with inconceivable speed, yet it is under His feet, beneath His perfect control!

- Look at God's power **in creation**. "The heavens are yours; the earth also is yours; the world and all that is in it, you have founded them. The north and the south, you have created them" (Ps. 89:11, 12). Before people can work, they must have tools and materials, but God began with nothing, and just by His word, things were made from nothing. Our intellect cannot grasp it. God "spoke, and it came to be; he commanded, and it stood firm" (Ps. 33:9). Primeval matter heard His voice. "God said, 'Let there be…' and it was so" (Gen 1). That would make us say,

"You have a mighty arm; strong is your hand, high your right hand" (Ps. 89:13).

Whoever looks at the midnight sky and sees all its wonders, cannot stop asking "What were these mighty planets and stars made out of?" It is amazing to think they were produced without materials. They came from emptiness. The fabric of universal nature emerged from nothing. What tools were used by the Supreme Architect to make everything such exquisite beauty, and give everything a wonderful polish? How was it all connected into one finely proportioned structure? One command accomplished it all. 'Let them be,' said God. He said nothing else, and immediately the marvelous creation arose, adorned with every beauty, displaying numerous perfections, and declaring praise of its Creator. "By the word of the Lord the heavens were made, and by the breath of his mouth all their host" (Ps. 33:6) (James Hervey, 1819).

- Look at God's power **in preservation**. No being or creature has the power to sustain itself. "Can papyrus grow where there is no marsh? Can reeds flourish where there is no water?" (Job 8:11). People and animals would die if there were no herbs for food. Herbs would wither and die if the earth was not refreshed with rain. So, God is the preserver of "man and beast" (Ps. 36:6). "He upholds the universe by the word of his power" (Heb 1:3). What incredible power is the pre-birth life of every human being! That a baby can live for so many months in cramped and filthy quarters, and do so without breathing, is inexplicable without the power of God. Truly He "has kept our soul among the living" (Ps. 66:9).

Preserving the earth from the violence of the sea is another example of God's might. How is that raging element kept within those limits that He first gave it, continuing without overflowing the earth and killing all creation? The natural position for water is to be above the earth, because it is lighter, and under the air, because it is heavier. Who maintains this natural quality? People do not, and cannot. It is the command of its Creator which controls it: "And said, 'Thus far shall you come, and no farther, and here shall your proud waves be stayed'?" (Job 38:11). What a monument to the power of God is the preservation of the world!

- Look at God's power **in government**. Look at how he restrained the hatred of Satan. "Your adversary the devil prowls around like a roaring lion, seeking someone to devour" (1 Pet. 5:8). He is filled with hatred for God and people, especially Christians. He envied Adam in paradise and envies the pleasure we have of enjoying God's blessings. If he had his way, he would treat us all the same way he treated Job: he would send fire on the crops and produce, destroy the cattle, cause a wind to destroy our houses, and cover our bodies with boils. But God bridles him to a large extent, prevents him from carrying out his evil designs, and confines him within His commands.

So, God also restrains the natural corruption of men. He suffers enough of our sin to allow the consequences of our turning away from our Maker, but who can imagine the horrible extent we would go to if God completely removed His hand of protection? "Their mouth is full of curses and bitterness. Their feet are swift to shed blood" (Rom. 3:14-15). This is the nature of every descendant of Adam. What uncontrolled immorality and foolishness would take over the world, if God's power did not intervene to lock down its floodgates (Ps. 93:3-4)?

- Look at God's power **in judgment**. When He strikes, no one can resist Him (Ez. 22:14). This was demonstrated in the Flood! God opened the windows of heaven and broke up the great fountains of the deep, and the entire human race (except those in the ark), were helpless before the storm of His judgment and were swept away. With a shower of fire and brimstone from heaven, the cities of the plain were exterminated. Pharaoh and his people were weak when God blew on them at the Red Sea.

Look at the word used in Romans 9:22: "What if God, desiring to show his wrath and to make known his power, has endured with much patience vessels of wrath prepared for destruction." God is going to display His mighty power on sinners not just by locking them up in Hell, but by supernaturally preserving their bodies and souls in the eternal Lake of Fire.

Responding to His Power

- We should **tremble** before such a God! To treat someone who can crush us easier than a moth with disrespect is suicidal. To defy the one clothed with omnipotence, who can tear us to pieces or throw us into Hell any moment, is the height of insanity. To put it plainly, it is wisdom to obey His command, "Kiss the Son, lest he be angry, and you perish in the way, for his wrath is quickly kindled. Blessed are all who take refuge in him" (Ps. 2:12).
- We should **adore** such a God! The wonderful and infinite perfections of such a Being demand worship. If strong, famous people are admired by the world, how much more should the power of the Almighty fill us with awe and worship? "Who is like you, O Lord, among the gods? Who is like you, majestic in holiness, awesome in glorious deeds, doing wonders? (Ex. 15:11).
- We should **trust** such a God! He is worthy of complete confidence. Nothing is too difficult for Him. If God were restricted in power and had a limit to His strength, then we should worry. But seeing Him clothed with omnipotence, no prayer is too difficult for Him to answer, no need too great for Him to supply, no passion too strong for Him to subdue, no temptation too powerful for Him to deliver from, no misery too deep for Him to relieve. "The Lord is the stronghold of my life; of whom shall I be afraid?" (Ps. 27:1).

Now to him who is able to do far more abundantly than all that we ask or think, according to the power at work within us, to him be glory in the church and in Christ Jesus throughout all generations, forever and ever. Amen. (Eph 3:20,-21)

Reflections

The Old Testament is filled with anecdotes of God's immense power: seas parting, mountains. splitting, burning bushes, and the sun stopping. They are vast exhibitions of His tremendous control over nature. Even the people refused to go up the mountain, sending Moses ahead because they were terrified of His power that raged and rumbled overhead. The contest between Baal and God ended with Elijah calling down fire from heaven to obliterate the altar. But the New Testament sees more intimate miracles and occurrences of God's power. He does not stop being all-powerful and omnipotent but focuses on our hearts, the inner man, rather than manifesting through creation.

1. Do you have more of an Old or New Testament view of God's power? Are they different or the same?
2. Have you ever experienced God's power in some way? When and how?
3. Why is God's power important to us as Christians?
4. Read Romans 8:31. Why is this such a helpful verse for us when we face tough times?

10

THE FAITHFULNESS OF GOD

In All Things, At All Times

Unfaithfulness is one of the most common sins of our time. In the business world, a person's word is no longer their bond. In the social world, marital infidelity is on the rise, and the sacred bonds of wedlock are broken as quickly as discarding old clothes. In the spiritual realm, thousands who have promised to preach the truth have no hesitation in attacking and denying it. None of us are immune to this terrible sin. How many ways have we been unfaithful to Jesus and to the light and blessings God has given us?

How refreshing it is to lift our eyes above all this decay and see someone who is faithful—in all things, at all times.

"Know therefore that the Lord your God is God, the faithful God" (Deut. 7:9). This quality is essential to His being; without it, He would not be God. For God to be unfaithful would be contrary to His nature, which is impossible. "If we are faithless, he remains faithful— for he cannot deny himself" (2 Tim. 2:13). Faithfulness is one of the glorious perfections of His being. He is clothed with it: "O LORD God of hosts, who is mighty as you are, O LORD, with your faithfulness all around you?" (Ps. 89:8). And when God became a man: "Righteousness shall be the belt of his waist, and faithfulness the belt of his loins" (Isa. 11:5).

"Your steadfast love, O Lord, extends to the heavens, your faithfulness to the clouds" (Ps. 36:5). Far above all human understanding is the unchanging faithfulness of God. Everything about God is great, vast, incomparable. He never forgets, never fails, never falters, never forfeits His word. To every promise or prophecy, the Lord has remained true. Every covenant or threat, He will accomplish, because "God is not man, that he should lie, or a son of man, that he should change his mind. Has he said, and will he not do it? Or has he spoken, and will he not fulfill it?" (Num. 23:19).

That is why believers say, "The steadfast love of the Lord never ceases; his mercies never come to an end" (Lam. 3:22-23).

The Bible is filled with examples of God's faithfulness. More than four thousand years ago He said, "While the earth remains, seedtime and harvest, cold and heat, summer and winter, day and night, shall not cease" (Gen. 8:22). Every year is a fresh witness to God's fulfillment of this promise.

Jehovah said to Abraham, "Your offspring will be sojourners in a land that is not theirs and will be servants there... And they shall come back here in the fourth generation" (Gen.

15:13-16). Many centuries passed as Abraham's descendants groaned working the brick kilns of Egypt. Had God forgotten His promise? No. "At the end of 430 years, on that very day, all the hosts of the LORD went out from the land of Egypt" (Ex. 12:41).

Through Isaiah, the Lord said, "Behold, the virgin shall conceive and bear a son, and shall call his name Immanuel" (Isa. 7:14). Again, centuries passed, but "When the fullness of time had come, God sent forth his Son, born of woman" (Gal 4:4).

God is true. His promise is sure. In all His dealings with His people, God is faithful. He can be relied upon. No one ever trusted Him in vain. This is shown almost everywhere in the Bible, because His people need to know that faithfulness is an essential part of His character. This is the basis of our confidence in Him.

But it is one thing to accept the faithfulness of God as truth, and quite another to act on it. God has given us many "precious and very great promises" (2 Pet. 1:4), but are we really counting on Him fulfilling them? Are we actually **expecting** Him to do everything He has said? Are we resting on the assurance of these words: "he who promised is faithful" (Heb. 10:23)?

In Hard Times

There are seasons in our lives when it is not easy to believe that God is faithful, even for Christians. Our faith is tested, our eyes are blurred with tears, and we can no longer see His love at work. Our ears are distracted by the noises of the world, harassed by the atheistic whispers of Satan, and we can no longer hear His still small voice. Our plans have failed, friends have deserted us, and a brother or sister in Christ has betrayed us. We are staggered. We tried to be faithful to God, and now a dark cloud hides Him from us. We find it difficult, almost impossible, to see harmony in His frowning provision and His gracious promises. We need to find grace in this verse: "Who among you fears the Lord and obeys the voice of his servant? Let him who walks in darkness and has no light" (Isa. 50:10).

When you are tempted to doubt the faithfulness of God, shout, "Get behind me, Satan." Even though you cannot harmonize God's mysterious dealings with His promised love, wait on Him for more light. In His own time, He will make it clear to you. "What I am doing you do not understand now, but afterward you will understand" (John 13:7). What happens next will demonstrate that God has not forsaken or deceived His child. "Therefore the Lord waits to be gracious to you, and therefore he exalts himself to show mercy to you. For the Lord is a God of justice; blessed are all those who wait for him" (Isa. 30:18).

Judge not the Lord by feeble sense,

But trust Him for His grace,

Behind a frowning providence

He hides a smiling face.

Ye fearful saints, fresh courage take,

The clouds ye so much dread,

Are rich with mercy, and shall break

In blessing o'er your head (Cowper, n.d.).

"You have appointed your testimonies in righteousness and in all faithfulness" (Ps. 119:138). God has not only told us the best, but He has not hidden the worst. He has faithfully described the devastation caused by the Fall. He has faithfully diagnosed the terrible state sin has produced. He has faithfully made His hatred of evil known, and that He must punish it. He has faithfully warned us that He is "a consuming fire" (Heb. 12:29). Not only is His Word filled with examples of Him fulfilling His promises, but it also records many instances of Him carrying out His threats. Every stage of Israel's history demonstrates this. So it was with people: Pharaoh, Korah, Achan, and many others are proof of it. And it will be like that with us. Unless you have run or are running to Jesus for refuge, the everlasting burning of the Lake of Fire is where you will end. God is faithful.

Faithfulness Demonstrated

- God is faithful in **preserving** His people. "God is faithful, by whom you were called into the fellowship of his Son, Jesus Christ our Lord" (1 Cor. 1:9). In the verse before, a promise was made that God would confirm to the end. Paul's confidence in the security of believers was not based on the strength of their resolutions or ability to persevere but on the reliability of God who cannot lie. Since God has promised to His Son a chosen people for His inheritance, to deliver them from sin and condemnation, and to make them participants of eternal life in glory, it is certain that He will not allow any of them to perish.

- God is faithful in **disciplining** His people. He is faithful in what He denies us as well as in what He gives us. He is faithful in sending sorrow as well as in giving joy. The faithfulness of God is a truth we can declare when we are comfortable, but also when we are struggling under the sharpest rebuke. It is a confession not just from our mouths, but of our hearts, too. When God beats us with the rod of discipline, it is faithfulness He uses. To acknowledge this means we humble ourselves before Him, admit we deserve His correction, and instead of complaining, thank Him for it.

God never brings trouble without a reason. "That is why many of you are weak and ill, and some have died" (1 Cor 11:30), says Paul to explain this principle. When His rod falls on us, let us say, "To you, O LORD, belongs righteousness, but to us open shame" (Dan. 9:7).

"I know, O Lord, that your rules are righteous, and that in faithfulness you have afflicted me" (Ps. 119:75). Trouble and hardship are not only consistent with God's promised love in the everlasting covenant, but they are ways of showing and administering it. God is not only faithful when there are no hardships, but faithful in sending them. "Then I will punish their transgression with the rod and their iniquity with stripes, but I will not remove from him my steadfast love or be false to my faithfulness" (Ps. 89:32-33). Discipline is not only part of God's loving-kindness, it is its effect and expression. It would ease our worries if we remembered that His covenant love requires Him to discipline us. Hardships are necessary: "In their distress earnestly seek me" (Hos. 5:15).

- God is faithful in **glorifying** His people. "He who calls you is faithful; he will surely do it," refers to the saints being "kept blameless at the coming of our Lord Jesus Christ" (1 Thess. 5:23-24). God does not deal with us on our merits (for we have none) but for His own name's sake. God is constant to Himself and to His own purpose of grace, "those whom he justified he also glorified" (Rom. 8:30). God demonstrates the consistency of His goodness toward His chosen people by calling them out of darkness into His marvelous light, and this should convince them of its continuation. "But God's firm foundation stands" (2 Tim. 2:19). Paul was resting on the faithfulness of God when he said, "I know whom I have believed, and I am convinced that he is able to guard until that day what has been entrusted to me" (2 Tim. 1:12).

Faith in His Faithfulness

- Understanding this truth will **keep us from worry**. To be full of anxiety, to view our situation with dark fears, and to anticipate tomorrow with nervousness, reflects badly on the faithfulness of God. He who has taken care of His children through all the years will not forsake them in their old age. He who has heard your prayers in the past will not refuse to supply your needs in the present emergency. Rest on Job 5:19, "He will deliver you from six troubles; in seven no evil shall touch you."

- Understanding this truth will **stop our complaints**. The Lord knows what is best for each one of us, and one effect of resting on this truth is the silencing of our complaints. God is honored when, under trial and discipline, we have good thoughts of Him, defend His wisdom and justice, and recognize His love in His rebukes.
- Understanding this truth will **increase our confidence in God**. "Therefore let those who suffer according to God's will entrust their souls to a faithful Creator while doing good" (1 Pet. 4:19). When we surrender everything into God's hands, persuaded of His love and faithfulness, then we will be satisfied with His provision and realize that He does all things well.

Reflections

God's faithfulness is one of His most endearing attributes. It is one most Christians hold onto in tough times, when they are down, and when they have backslidden. To be able to trust in a God who never fails, and who sticks to His promises, no matter what, has kept many of us afloat. If it was not for faithfulness, then we would all be lost at sea, drifting endlessly with no hope. God's faithfulness is not just an attribute on its own but sustains many of His other characteristics. We can rely on His patience, love, mercy, power, and grace because He will never fail in any of these. He will remain true!

1. Why is faithfulness such a rare quality in the world?
2. Read 2 Timothy 2:13. What does this verse mean to you?
3. Read Hebrews 13:5. What does this mean in the context of God's faithfulness?
4. What does faith have to do with faithfulness?
5. Read Lamentations 3:22–23. Does this encourage you in any way?

11

THE GOODNESS OF GOD

Goodness Revealed

The steadfast love of God endures (Ps. 52:1). The goodness of God refers to the perfection of His nature: "God is light, and in him is no darkness at all" (1 John 1:5). There is such perfection in God's nature and being that nothing is lacking or defective in it, and nothing can be added to it to make it better. Thomas Manton said:

He is good in Himself, which nothing else is because all creatures are only good because of their connection to God. He is essentially good; not only good, but goodness itself. The created being's good is a super-added quality, whereas in God it is His essence. He is infinitely good; the creature's good is but a drop, but in God there is an infinite ocean of good. He is eternally and immutably good because He cannot be less good than He is; as there can be no addition made to Him, so no subtraction from Him. (Musselman, 2023)

God is the highest good.

The original meaning of the English word God is "The Good." God is not only the greatest of all beings, but the best. All the goodness in any creature has come from the Creator, but God's goodness is unmatched because it is the essence of His eternal nature. Just as God was infinite in power before eternity, and before His omnipotence was shown, so He was eternally good before there was any pouring out of His blessings or any creature lived to whom it might be given. The first display was in giving life to all things. "You are good and do good; teach me your statutes" (Ps. 119:68). God has in Himself an infinite treasure of all goodness, enough to fill all things.

Everything that comes from God—decrees, creation, laws, provision—cannot be anything but good. As it is written, "God saw everything that he had made, and behold, it was very good" (Gen. 1:31).

So, the goodness of God is first seen in creation. The more closely the creature is studied, the more the generosity of its Creator becomes apparent. Take the highest of God's earthly creatures—humans. There are plenty of reasons to say, "I praise you, for I am fearfully and wonderfully made. Wonderful are your works; my soul knows it very well" (Ps. 139:14). Everything about the structure of our bodies shows the goodness of their Maker. He made our hands capable of performing their tasks! He gave us sleep to refresh our tired bodies! He generously made lids and brows to protect the eyes! We can continue listing all the wonderful parts of the body.

The goodness of the Creator is not just confined to humans, it extends to all His creatures. "The eyes of all look to you, and you give them their food in due season. You open your hand; you satisfy the desire of every living thing" (Ps. 145:15-16). Books can and have been written about this. Whether it is the birds of the air, the beasts of the forest, or the fish in the sea, abundant provision has been made to supply all their needs. God is "He who gives food to all flesh, for his steadfast love endures forever" (Ps. 136:25). "The earth is full of the steadfast love of the Lord" (Ps. 33:5).

The goodness of God is seen in the variety of natural pleasures which He has provided for His creatures. God might have been pleased to satisfy our hunger without the food pleasing our palates—how generous He is to provide varied flavors to meats, vegetables, and fruits! God has not only given us senses but also things that please them, again revealing His goodness. The earth might have been as fertile as it is without being so beautifully decorated. Our physical lives could have been sustained without beautiful flowers to entertain our eyes with their colors, and our nostrils with their sweet perfumes. We might have walked in the fields without our ears being filled with the music of birds. Where does all this beauty come from that is so freely poured out over nature? They are the tender mercies of the Lord "over all that he has made" (Ps. 145:9).

The goodness of God is seen when people broke the law of their Creator, after which anger and judgment did not immediately start. God could have deprived His fallen creatures of every blessing, comfort, and pleasure. Instead, He supplied mercy mixed with judgment. It is incredible to examine this dual existence, especially when we look closely and see that "mercy triumphs over judgment" (James 2:13). Despite all the evil of our fallen state, the balance of good dominates. Generally, men and women experience more days of health than they do of sickness and pain. There is more happiness than misery in the world.

The generosity of God cannot be questioned because there is suffering and sorrow in the world. If people sin against the goodness of God and despise "the riches of his kindness and forbearance and patience," and because of their hard, unrepentant hearts, they heap up hatred against the day of judgment (Rom. 2:4-5), who is to blame but themselves? Would God be good if He did not punish those who misuse His blessings, abuse His generosity, and trample His mercies beneath their feet? It is no reflection on God's goodness, but rather the clearest illustration of it, when He clears the earth of those who have broken His laws, defied His authority, mocked His messengers, scorned His Son, and persecuted those for whom He died.

The goodness of God was shown very clearly when He sent His Son "born of woman, born under the law, to redeem those who were under the law, so that we might receive adoption as sons" (Gal. 4:4-5). The angels praised their Maker and said, "Glory to God in the highest, and on earth peace among those with whom he is pleased!" (Luke 2:14). The grace of God has appeared, bringing salvation for all people (Titus 2:11). God's compassion cannot be called into question because He has not made every sinful creature subject of His redemptive grace. He did not do it to the fallen angels. If God had left everyone to die, it would not have been a reflection of His goodness. To anyone challenging this statement, we will remind them of God's prerogative and privilege: "Am I not allowed to do what I choose with what belongs to me? Or do you begrudge my generosity?" (Matt. 20:15).

Praise Him for His Goodness

"Let them thank the Lord for his steadfast love, for his wondrous works to the children of man!" (Ps. 107:8). Gratitude is the response to His generosity, yet it is often not given, simply because His goodness is so constant and so abundant. It is taken for granted because it is given to us in the most common ways. It is not felt because we experience it every day. "Do you despise the riches of His goodness" (Rom 2:4, NKJV). His goodness is despised when it does not lead us to repentance but hardens us to think that God overlooks our sins.

The goodness of God is the life of a Christian's trust. This appeals most to our hearts. Because His goodness endures forever, we should never be discouraged: "The Lord is good, a stronghold in the day of trouble; he knows those who take refuge in him" (Nah. 1:7).

When others behave badly to us, it should only stir us up the more heartily to give thanks unto the Lord, because He is good; and when we ourselves are conscious that we are far from being good, we should only the more reverently bless

Him that He is good. We must never tolerate an instant's unbelief as to the goodness of the Lord; whatever else may be questioned, this is absolutely certain, that Jehovah is good; His dispensations may vary, but His nature is always the same (Spurgeon, 2024).

Reflections

Although most of us believe God is good in principle, when things are not going well, we tend to think otherwise (even if it's secretly to ourselves). Our idea of good is when everything is going without a hitch, with no problems. We balance everything bad versus everything good and rank God according to that list. But God's idea of good transcends our emotional, selfish outlook. He is good overall, ensuring that the world does not totally fall apart and that we are still in His hands—even in illness, hardship, and death. The reality is that God's goodness is not purely physical, but intent on our spiritual good. While He cares for our needs, it is not His main concern: our hearts are His end goal.

1. If you were brutally honest, and rated God on how good you think He is, what would you give Him out of 10? Why?
2. Why do people (Christians and non-Christians) have problems seeing God as completely good?
3. Read Psalm 119:68. Do you agree with all of this verse?
4. Is there a difference between an optimistic view of things and spiritually seeing God and everything He does as good?

12

THE PATIENCE OF GOD

A lot less has been written on this than the other attributes, many passing over the patience of God without any comment. There is no reason for this because the longsuffering of God is as much one of the attributes as is His wisdom, power, or holiness—to be admired and revered by us. The term is not in a Bible concordance as frequently as the others, but its glory shines on almost every page of the Bible. We lose out if we do not meditate on the patience of God and pray that our hearts and ways may be more completely conformed to it.

Maybe the reason why so many writers skipped the patience of God was because of the difficulty of distinguishing this attribute from His goodness and mercy. God's longsuffering is mentioned with His grace and mercy again and again (Ex. 34:6, Num. 14:18, Ps. 86:15, etc.). We cannot deny that the patience of God is really a display of His mercy. However, we cannot accept that patience and mercy are the same attributes. It may not be easy to separate them, but the Bible confirms some things about the one which we cannot agree on about the other.

His Patience Endures

Stephen Charnock (1840), the Puritan, defines God's patience like this:

It is part of God's goodness and mercy yet differs from both. God being the greatest goodness, has the greatest gentleness; gentleness is always the companion of true goodness, and the greater the goodness, the greater the gentleness. Who is so holy as Christ, and who is so meek? God's slowness to anger is a branch... from His mercy: "The Lord is gracious and merciful, slow to anger and abounding in steadfast love" (Ps. 145:8). It differs from mercy in considering the object: mercy respects the creature as miserable, patience respects the creature as criminal; mercy pities him in his misery, and patience bears with the sin which caused the misery, and is giving birth to more.

We could define His patience as that power of control that God exercises over Himself, causing Him to bear with the wicked and refrain from punishing them. "The Lord is slow to anger and great in power" (Nah. 1:3). So, Stephen Charnock said:

Men that are great in the world are quick in passion and are not so ready to forgive an injury, or bear with an offender, as one of a lesser rank. It is a lack of power over that man's self that makes him do improper things on impulse. A prince who can bridle his passions is a king over himself as well as over his subjects. God is slow to anger because He is great in power. He has no less power over Himself than over His creatures.

This is how God's patience is most clearly distinguished from His mercy. Even though the creature benefits from it, the patience of God respects Himself, a restraint on His actions by His will, whereas His mercy ends completely on the creature. The patience of God is that attribute that causes Him to put up with things without immediately avenging Himself. He has a power of patience as well as a power of justice.

The Hebrew word for God's long-suffering is "slow to anger" (Neh. 9:17, Ps. 103:8, etc.). Not that there are any passions or emotions in God's nature, but that God's wisdom and will are pleased to act according to His majesty. To support this definition, we see Moses appealing to God's patience when Israel sinned at Kadesh-Barnea and provoked Jehovah. The Lord said, "I will strike them with the pestilence and disinherit them" (Num. 14:12). Then Moses mediated, as a type of Jesus, and pleaded, "And now, please let the power of the Lord be great as you have promised, saying, 'The Lord is slow to anger" (Num 14:17-18). His patience and long-suffering are revealed through His power of self-restraint.

"What if God, desiring to show his wrath and to make known his power, has endured with much patience vessels of wrath prepared for destruction" (Rom. 9:22). If God suddenly broke those condemned vessels into pieces, His power of self-control would not be evident. By bearing with their wickedness and holding off on punishment, the power of His patience is gloriously demonstrated. The wicked interpret His long-suffering quite differently—"Because the sentence against an evil deed is not executed speedily, the heart of the children of man is fully set to do evil" (Eccl. 8:11)—but the anointed eye adores what they abuse.

"The God of endurance and encouragement" is one of the divine titles (Rom. 15:5).

1. Deity is listed first because God is the Author and object of the grace of patience in Christians.
2. Secondly, because this is what He is in Himself: patience is one of His perfections.
3. Thirdly, as an example for us: "Put on then, as God's chosen ones, holy and beloved, compassionate hearts, kindness, humility, meekness, and patience" (Col 3:12). "Therefore be imitators of God, as beloved children" (Eph 5:1).

When we are tempted to be disgusted at the dullness of someone else or want revenge on a person who has wronged us, remember God's infinite patience and long-suffering with ourselves.

Then and Now

- God's patience is shown **in how He dealt with sinners**. Before the Flood, when people were degenerate and were all corrupted by their flesh, God did not destroy them until He had warned them. He "waited" (1 Pet. 3:20) for about 120 years (Gen 6:3), during which time Noah was a "herald of righteousness" (2 Pet. 2:5). Later, when the Gentiles worshiped and served the creature more than the Creator and committed terrible abominations contrary to nature, being filled with iniquity, God yet held back his sword (Rom. 1:19-26)

In past generations, he allowed all the nations to walk in their own ways. Yet he did not leave himself without witness, for he did good by giving you rains from heaven and fruitful seasons. (Acts 14:16-17)

- God's patience was shown **toward Israel**. First, He "put up with them for forty years in the wilderness" (Acts 13:18). Later, when they had entered Canaan, but followed the evil customs of the nations around them and turned to idolatry, even though God disciplined them, He did not completely destroy them but raised up deliverers for them. When their iniquity became so much that only a God of infinite patience could have tolerated them, He spared them many years before He allowed them to be carried down into Babylon. Finally, when their rebellion against Him reached its climax by crucifying His Son, He waited forty years before sending the Romans against them, only after they had judged themselves "unworthy of eternal life" (Acts 13:46).
- God's patience is shown **in how He deals with the world today**. Everywhere people are sinning without

a care. God's law is trampled underfoot, and God is openly despised. It is amazing that He does not instantly strike dead those who so brazenly defy Him. Why does He not suddenly cut off the proud unbeliever and blatant blasphemer, as He did with Ananias and Sapphira? Why does He not cause the earth to open and swallow the persecutors of His people, like Dathan and Abiram? And what of backslidden Christians, where every sin is now tolerated and practiced in the name of Jesus? Why does God's righteous judgment of Heaven bring such abominations to an end? Only one answer is possible: because God bears with "much patience vessels of wrath prepared for destruction" (Rom. 9:22).

And what about us? Let us look at our own lives. It was not long ago that we followed others in doing evil, had no concern for God's glory, and lived only to gratify ourselves. How patiently He tolerated our terrible behavior! And now that grace has snatched us from the burning fire, giving us a place in God's family, and adopted us into an eternal inheritance in glory, how badly we turn on Him. How shallow is our gratitude, how slow is our obedience, how frequent are our backslidings? One reason why God allows the flesh to remain in the believer is for Him to show His "patience toward you" (2 Pete.3:9). Since this attribute is shown only in this world, God takes advantage to display it toward His people.

Schooled in Patience

Our meditation on this attribute must soften our hearts, make our consciences tender, and help us to learn in the school of holy experience the patience of saints—submission to His will and persevering in doing good. Let us seek grace to imitate this attribute. "You therefore must be perfect, as your heavenly Father is perfect" (Matt. 5:48). In this verse, Jesus encourages us to love our enemies, bless those who curse us, and do good to those who hate us. God tolerates the wicked despite their many sins, and do we want revenge on someone else because of one small thing someone did against us?

Reflections

We seldom use the old-fashioned word longsuffering for patience, yet it expresses this attribute so well. God has, and will continue to suffer our weaknesses, failings, and erratic faith for a long time. Instead of reacting immediately to our futile attempts at being good Christians, He waits for us, knowing that it will take us some time before we finally submit to Him. This patience is an incredible quality, especially when we try and test it so often and so much. Without it, God would have expunged and expelled us a long, long time ago. But instead, He waits patiently like a good father would for his child to learn and come to a place of acceptance and maturity.

1. How does God show patience?
2. What does the phrase *"slow to anger"* mean to you?

3. Why is patience such a difficult quality for us as people to exhibit?
4. Read Psalm 37. Why is patience necessary when it comes to following God?
5. How can you learn to be patient from God's example?

13

THE GRACE OF GOD

A Perfection

Grace is a perfection of God's character exercised only toward His chosen people. The grace of God is never mentioned in connection with mankind, neither in the Old Testament nor in the New is generally, still less with the lower orders of His creatures. It is different from mercy because the mercy of God is "all that he has made" (Ps. 145:9). Grace is the sole source from which flows the goodwill, love, and salvation of God unto His chosen people. This attribute was defined by Abraham Booth in his book, *The Reign of Grace*: "It is the eternal and absolute free favor of God, manifested in the vouchsafement of spiritual and eternal blessings to the guilty and the unworthy" (1803).

God's grace is the sovereign and saving favor of God through blessings He gives those who do not deserve them and for which no payment is demanded. It is the favor of God shown to those who not only have no rewards of their own but who are hell-deserving. It is completely unmerited, unwarranted, and undeserved by anything in, from, or by those it is given to. Grace cannot be bought, earned, or won by us. If it could be, it would not be grace. When something is said to be of grace, we mean that the recipient has no claim on it, that it was not owed to him. It comes to him as pure charity, unasked and undesired.

The best description of God's amazing grace is found in Paul's letter. Grace is in direct opposition to works and worthiness of every type or degree. "But if it is by grace, it is no longer on the basis of works; otherwise grace would no longer be grace" (Rom. 11:6). Grace and works will never unite any more than an acid and an alkali. "For by grace you have been saved through faith. And this is not your own doing; it is the gift of God, not a result of works, so that no one may boast" (Eph. 2:8-9). The absolute favor of God cannot consist of human merit any more than oil and water will combine into one (Rom 4:4-5).

There are three characteristics of God's grace.

1. It is **eternal**. Grace was planned before it was given, purposed before it was imparted: "Who saved us and called us to a holy calling, not because of our works but because of his own purpose and grace, which he gave us in Christ Jesus before the ages began" (2 Tim. 1:9).
2. It is **free**. No one bought it: "And are justified by his grace as a gift, through the redemption that is in Christ Jesus" (Rom. 3:24).

3. It is **sovereign**. God uses and gives it to whom He pleases: "Grace also might reign" (Rom 5:21). If grace reigns then it is on the throne, and the occupant of the throne is sovereign. So, it is called "the throne of grace" (Heb. 4:16).

His Choice

Just because grace is unmerited favor, it must be used in a sovereign manner. That is why God says, "I will be gracious to whom I will be gracious" (Ex. 33:19). If God showed grace to all of Adam's descendants, people would think that He was righteously compelled to take them to heaven as compensation for allowing the human race to fall into sin. But God is under no obligation to any of His creatures, especially those who rebel against Him. Eternal life is a gift, therefore: it cannot be earned by good works or claimed as a right. Since salvation is a gift, who has any right to tell God whom He can give it to? It is not that He ever refuses this gift to any who seeks it, and according to the rules He has prescribed. No! He refuses no one who comes empty-handed. But if God uses His sovereign right by choosing a few to be saved out of a world of unrepentant and unbelieving rebels, who has been wronged? Is God obliged to force His gift on those who do not value it? Is God compelled to save those who are determined to go their own way? Nothing irritates unbelievers and reveals their hatred of God more than emphasizing the eternality, freeness, and sovereignty of His grace. That God should have formed His purpose before the earth, without consulting the creature, is too degrading for the unbroken heart.

The fact that grace cannot be earned or won by any efforts of man is too self-emptying for self-righteousness. And because grace singles out whom it pleases to be its favored recipients, that incites many protests from proud rebels. The clay rises up against the Potter and asks, "Why have You made me like this?" A lawless rebel dares to question the justice of God's sovereignty.

The distinguishing grace of God is seen in saving those people whom He has sovereignly singled out to be His favorites. By 'distinguishing,' we mean that grace discriminates, makes differences, chooses some, and passes by others. It was distinguishing grace that selected Abraham from his idolatrous neighbors and made him "a friend of God" (Jam. 2:23). It was distinguishing grace that saved tax collectors and sinners, but when it came to the religious Pharisees, said "Let them alone" (Matt 15:14). Nowhere does the glory of God's free and sovereign grace shine more brightly than in the unworthiness and unlikeliness of its recipients. James Hervey illustrated it best:

Where sin has abounded, says the proclamation from the court of heaven, grace abounds much more. Manasseh was a monster of barbarity, for he caused his own children to pass through the fire and filled Jerusalem with innocent blood. Manasseh was an adept in iniquity, for he not only multiplied, and to an extravagant degree, his own sacrilegious impieties, but he poisoned the principles and perverted the manners of his subjects, making them do worse than the most detestable of the heathen idolaters (2 Chron. 33). Yet, through this superabundant grace he is humbled, he is reformed and becomes a child of forgiving love, an heir of immortal glory.

Look at that bitter and bloody persecutor, Saul; when he was breathing out threats and bent on slaughter, he worried the lambs and put to death the disciples of Jesus. The havoc he had committed, the inoffensive families he had already ruined, were not sufficient to assuage his vengeful spirit. They were only a taste, which, instead of glutting the bloodhound, made him more closely pursue the track, and more eagerly pant for destruction. He still thirsted for violence and murder. So eager and insatiable is his thirst, that he even breathes out threats and slaughter (Acts 9:1). His words are spears and arrows, and his tongue a sharp sword. 'Tis as natural for him to menace the Christians as to breathe the air. They bled every hour for the purposes of his rancorous heart. It is only owing to lack of power that every syllable he utters, every breath he draws, does not deal out deaths, and cause some of the innocent disciples to fall.

Who would not have pronounced him a vessel of wrath, destined to unavoidable damnation? Who would not have been ready to conclude that, if there were heavier chains and a deeper dungeon in the world of woe, they must surely be reserved for such an implacable enemy of true godliness? Yet, admire and adore the inexhaustible treasures of grace—this Saul is admitted into the fellowship of the prophets, is numbered with the noble army of martyrs, and makes a distinguished figure among the glorious company of the apostles.

The Corinthians were shamefully wicked. Some of them wallowed in such abominable vices, and habituated themselves to such outrageous acts of injustice, as were a reproach to human nature. Yet even these sons of violence and slaves of sensuality were washed, sanctified, and justified (1 Cor. 6:9-11). "Washed," in the precious blood of a dying Redeemer; "sanctified," by the powerful operations of the blessed Spirit; "justified," through the infinitely tender mercies of a gracious God. Those who were once the burden of the earth are now the joy of heaven, the delight of angels (Hervey, 1819).

Now the grace of God is revealed "in and by and through the Lord Jesus Christ. 'For the law was given through Moses; grace and truth came through Jesus Christ'" (John 1:17). This does not mean God never showed grace to anyone before His Son came to earth, as Genesis 6:8, Exodus 33:19, etc., clearly show otherwise. But grace and truth were fully revealed and perfectly demonstrated when the Redeemer came to this earth and died for His people on the cross. It is through Jesus the Mediator that the grace of God flows to His chosen people.

Much more have the grace of God and the free gift by the grace of that one man Jesus Christ... much more will those who receive the abundance of grace and the free gift of righteousness reign in life through the one man Jesus Christ... so grace also might reign through righteousness leading to eternal life through Jesus Christ our Lord (Rom 5:15, 17, 21).

The grace of God is proclaimed in the Gospel—to the self-righteous Jew, a stumbling block, and to the conceited and philosophizing Greek, foolishness (Acts 20:24). Why?

Because there is nothing in it that gratifies the pride of man. Unless we are saved by grace, we cannot be saved at all. It declares that apart from Jesus, the gift of God's grace, every person's state is desperate, irremediable, and hopeless. The Gospel addresses people as guilty, condemned, perishing criminals. It declares that the most moral person is in the same terrible situation as the most sinful sinner. The zealous Christian, with all his religious performances, is no better off than the most wicked unbeliever.

The Gospel sees every descendant of Adam as a fallen, polluted, hell-deserving, and helpless sinner. The grace that the Gospel offers is our only hope. We stand before God convicted as transgressors of His holy law, as guilty and condemned criminals, not just awaiting sentence, but the execution of the sentence already passed down (John 3:18, Rom. 3:19). To complain against the partiality of grace is suicidal. If the sinner insists upon pure justice, then the Lake of Fire is their eternal reward. Their only hope lies in bowing to the sentence that justice has passed down, owning the righteousness of it, throwing themselves on the mercy of God, and stretching empty hands out to receive the grace of God revealed to them in the Gospel.

The third person in the Godhead transmits grace; therefore, He is called "the Spirit of grace" (Zech. 12:10).

- God the Father is the fountain of all grace because He purposed in Himself the everlasting covenant of redemption.
- God the Son is the only channel of grace.
- The Gospel declares grace.

- The Holy Spirit is the transmitter and communicator. He is the one who applies the Gospel in saving power to the soul: renewing the chosen while spiritually dead, conquering their rebellious wills, melting their hard hearts, opening their blind eyes, cleansing them from the sickness of sin.

That is why G.S. Bishop (1912) said:

Grace is a provision for men who are so fallen that they cannot lift the axe of justice, so corrupt that they cannot change their own natures, so averse to God that they cannot turn to Him, so blind that they cannot see Him, so deaf that they cannot hear Him, and so dead that He Himself must open their graves and lift them into resurrection.

Reflections

God's grace has been an issue that the church has fallen hard on, resulting in Christians willfully living their lives because they see it as a get-out-of-jail-free card, or throwing it out completely and reverting back to the law. The Romans and Galatians struggled with both sides of the issue and needed correction. The truth is God's grace is incredibly important, especially under the New Covenant that we live under. Seeing God's grace in sending Jesus to die for us is a key element to living a Christian life of freedom in Christ. While it is a free gift to us undeserving sinners, it is not to be misused for our own benefit. It is for us to grow and walk in fullness with Him.

1. What is your definition of grace?
2. Have you, or do you feel God's grace in your life?
3. How did Jesus bring grace to us? Read John 1:16–17 and Ephesians 2:8–9.
4. Why is it so hard for us to accept grace as a free gift; why do we always fall into performing works to gain God's favor?

14

THE MERCY OF GOD

Mercy From Goodness

"Give thanks to the Lord, for he is good, for his steadfast love endures forever" (Ps. 136:1). For this attribute of God is to be praised. Three times in as many verses the Psalmist calls on the people to give thanks to the Lord for this attribute. It is the least that is asked of us who have received such treasure. When we think of the characteristics of mercy, we can only bless God for it. His mercy is "great" (1 Kings 3:6), "abounding" (Ps. 86:5), "tender" (Luke 1:78), "abundant" (1 Pet. 1:3, NKJV), and is from "everlasting to everlasting on those who fear him" (Ps. 103:17). We can say, "I will sing of your strength" (Ps. 59:16). "I will make all my goodness pass before you and will proclaim before you my name 'The Lord.' And I will be gracious to whom I will be gracious, and will show mercy on whom I will show mercy" (Ex. 33:19).

What is the difference between the mercy and grace of God? The mercy of God springs from goodness. The first gift of God's goodness is his generosity, which makes Him give abundantly to His creatures, so He gave life to all things. The second gift of God's goodness is His mercy, which is God's inclination to relieve the misery of fallen people. So, mercy assumes sin.

Even though it may not be easy at first to see a real difference between the grace and the mercy of God, it helps us if we look carefully at how He dealt with the unfallen angels. He has never shown mercy toward them, because they never needed it, since they had not sinned or come under the effects of the curse. They are still the recipients of God's free and sovereign grace

1. because of His **election** of them from out of all the angels (1 Tim. 5:21);
2. because of His **preservation** of them from turning away, when Satan rebelled and dragged one-third of the celestial hosts down with him (Rev. 12:4);
3. in making Christ their **Head** (Col. 2:10; I Pet. 3:22), they are eternally secured in the holy condition in which they were created; and
4. because of the exalted **position** assigned to them: to live in God's immediate presence (Dan. 7:10), to constantly serve Him in His heavenly temple, to receive honorable duties from Him (Heb. 1:14). This is abundant grace toward them, but not mercy.

In trying to study the mercy of God in the Bible, a triple distinction needs to be made.

1. There is a **general** mercy of God, extended to all people, believers and unbelievers alike, as well as to the entire creation: "His mercy is over all that he has made" (Ps. 145:9); "he himself gives to all mankind life and breath and everything" (Acts 17:25). God has pity on creation and supplies it with suitable provision.
2. There is a **special** mercy of God given to people, helping and comforting them, despite their sins. To them, He also gives all the necessities of life: "For he makes his sun rise on the evil and on the good, and sends rain on the just and on the unjust" (Matt. 5:45).
3. There is a **sovereign** mercy reserved for the heirs of salvation, given to them in a covenant, through the Mediator.

Showing Mercy

Looking more at the difference between the special and sovereign mercies, it is important to note that the mercies God gives to the wicked are temporary—confined strictly to this present life. There will be no mercy extended to them beyond the grave: "For this is a people without discernment; therefore he who made them will not have compassion on them; he who formed them will show them no favor" (Isa. 27:11).

You might find this contradictory since the Bible says that "his steadfast love endures forever" (Ps. 136:1). Two things need to be pointed out: God can never stop being merciful, for this is a quality of the divine essence (Ps. 116:5), but exercising His mercy by His sovereign will. There is nothing outside Himself that forces Him to act. If there was, that thing would be supreme, and God would no longer be God. It is only sovereign grace that determines the exercise of divine mercy. God says so clearly: "For he says to Moses, 'I will have mercy on whom I have mercy'" (Rom. 9:15). It is not the wretchedness of the creature that causes Him to show mercy, because God is not influenced by anything outside of Himself as we are. If God was influenced by the misery of sick sinners, He would cleanse and save them all. But He does not. Why? Simply because it is not His pleasure and purpose to do so.

It also has nothing to do with the merits of the creatures that cause Him to pour mercies on them because it is a contradiction to speak of deserving mercy. "He saved us, not because of works done by us in righteousness, but according to his own mercy" (Titus 3:5)—the one standing in direct opposition to the other. The merit of Jesus is not what moves God to pour out mercies on His chosen people: that would be substituting the effect for the cause. It is through or because of the tender mercy of our God that Jesus was sent to His people (Luke 1:78). The merits of Jesus make it possible for God to righteously give spiritual mercies to His people, justice having been fully satisfied by Jesus as a guarantee! Mercy only comes from God's pleasure.

Who Receives His Mercy?

While God's mercy "endures forever," we must carefully observe the recipients to whom His mercy is shown. Even throwing the sinner into the Lake of Fire is an act of mercy. The punishment of the wicked can be seen from three angles.

1. From God's side, it is an act of **justice**, vindicating His honor. The mercy of God cannot distort His holiness and righteousness.
2. From their side, it is an act of **impartiality**, because they must suffer the reward of their sins.
3. But from the standpoint of the redeemed, the punishment of the wicked is an act of unspeakable **mercy**. How terrible if the children of God were forced to live in the midst of the children of the Devil forever! Heaven would immediately stop being heaven if Christians still heard the blasphemous and filthy language of the sinner. What a mercy that in the New Jerusalem "nothing unclean will ever enter it, nor anyone who does what is detestable or false" (Rev. 21:27)!

Before you think this is all fantasy and imagination, let us look at the Bible to support what has been said.

- "And in your [mercy] you will cut off my enemies, and you will destroy all the adversaries of my soul, for I am your servant" (Ps. 143:12).
- God "overthrew Pharaoh and his host in the Red Sea, for his [mercy] endures forever." (Ps. 136:15). It was

an act of vengeance on Pharaoh and his people, but it was an act of mercy to the Israelites.

I heard what seemed to be the loud voice of a great multitude in heaven, crying out,

"Hallelujah!

Salvation and glory and power belong to our God,

for his judgments are true and just;

for he has judged the great prostitute

who corrupted the earth with her immorality,

and has avenged on her the blood of his servants.

Once more they cried out,

"Hallelujah!

The smoke from her goes up forever and ever." (Rev. 19:1-3)

Now we can see how useless the arrogant hope of the wicked is, who continue to defy God, and at the same time, still count on Him being merciful to them. There are many that say, "I do not believe that God will ever throw me into Hell; He is too merciful." Such a hope is a snake that will sting them to death if they continue to hold onto it. God is a God of justice as well as mercy, and He has clearly said that He will "by no means clear the guilty" (Ex. 34:7). He has also said, "The wicked shall return to Sheol, all the nations that forget God" (Ps. 9:17).

People might even go so far as to say, "I do not believe that if pollution be allowed to gather and sewage become stagnant and people deprive themselves of fresh air, that a merciful God will let them catch a deadly fever." The fact is that if you disregard the laws of health, you will contract a disease, despite God's mercy. It is also true that those who neglect the laws of spiritual health will suffer the second death forever.

It is serious to see so many abusing this attribute of mercy. They continue to despise God's authority, trample on His laws, continue in sin, and yet lean on His mercy. But God will not be unjust to Himself. God shows mercy to the truly repentant, but not to the impenitent (Luke 13:3). To continue in sin and rely on God's mercy to cancel out punishment is diabolical. It is like saying, "Why not do evil that good may come," but for them, their "condemnation is just" (Rom. 3:8). Presumption will certainly be disappointed (Deut. 29:18-20). Christ is the spiritual mercy seat, and all who despise and reject Him as Lord will "perish in the way, for his wrath is quickly kindled." (Ps. 2:12).

But let us look at God's spiritual mercies to His own people. "For your steadfast love is great to the heavens" (Ps. 57:10). Those riches transcend our highest thoughts. "For as high as the heavens are above the earth, so great is his steadfast love toward those who fear him;" (Ps. 103:11). No one can measure it. The chosen are called "vessels of mercy" (Rom. 9:23). It is mercy that gave them life when they were dead in sins (Eph. 2:4-5). It is mercy that saves them (Tit. 3:5). It is His abundant mercy which adopted them into an eternal inheritance (1 Pet. 1:3). We do not have enough time to express all His preserving, sustaining, pardoning, supplying mercy. He is "the Father of mercies" (2 Cor. 1:3).

When all Thy mercies, O my God,

My rising soul surveys,

Transported with the view I'm lost,

In wonder, love, and praise.

Reflections

As Pink points out, Jehovah is a merciful God and stands alone amongst the angry deities that must all be appeased. Many of us only see Him as angry and vengeful, especially when things go wrong so often. We think He is out to get us or we assume we have to do more to gain His favor. But when we delve into the Bible, we find He is not quick to thrust judgment on people, striking them down at will. Instead, we see a God who repeatedly warns those who are straying that they may come back and avoid the discipline that is to follow. He sent Jonah to warn Nineveh, and when they repented, the prophet was upset because he knew how merciful God would be to those wicked people if they turned to Him.

1. If he were only just and not also merciful, what could each of us reasonably expect from him?
2. What is the difference between mercy and grace?
3. Read Psalm 51:1 and 25:6. Why are mercy and steadfast love so closely linked?

4. Read Titus 3:3–8. How is receiving God's mercy linked with the power to live a new life?

15

THE LOVING-KINDNESS OF GOD

Let us look at another of God's attributes, one that every Christian has lots of proof of its existence. Analyzing His loving-kindness gives us balance so we do not have a biased view, the same way the Bible says, "God is light" and also "God is love" (1 John 1:5, 4:8). The stricter, more awe-inspiring aspects of God's character are counterbalanced by the gentler, more pleasant ones. We lose out if we focus exclusively on God's sovereignty and majesty, or His holiness and justice. We also need to meditate on His goodness and mercy. Nothing short of a clear view as revealed in the Bible will do.

A Multitude of Blessings

The Bible speaks of a "multitude of His loving-kindnesses," and who can count them all? (Isa. 63:7, NKJV). "How precious is Your lovingkindness, O God!" (Ps. 36:7). No human words, no angelic tongue, can adequately express it. While this attribute might be familiar to people, it is unique. None of the ancient gods were given such an endearing attribute as this. None of the idols worshiped by unbelievers possess gentleness and tenderness. The opposite is true, as the hideous features of their statues show. Philosophers see it as an honor to ascribe such severe qualities to a deity. But the Bible says a lot about God's loving-kindness, or His fatherly favor to His people, His tender affection toward them.

The first time this attribute is mentioned in the Bible is when God reveals Himself to Moses when Jehovah proclaimed His name. "The LORD, the LORD, a God merciful and gracious, slow to anger, and abounding in [loving-kindness] and faithfulness" (Ex. 34:6). The Hebrew word, *chesed*, is often translated as "kindness" and "loving-kindness." In our English Bibles, the initial mention is when David prayed, "Wondrously show[a] your steadfast love, O Savior of those who seek refuge from their adversaries at your right hand" (Ps. 17:7). How incredible that God who is so far above us, so inconceivably glorious, so deeply holy, should not only notice such worms of the earth but also set His heart on them, give His Son for them, send His Spirit to live in them and tolerate all their imperfections and disobedience to continue His loving-kindness to them.

Look at the evidence of how He has shown this attribute to His people:

- "In love he predestined us for adoption to himself as sons through Jesus Christ" (Eph. 1:4-5). That love

was engaged on their behalf before this world came into existence.
- "In this the love of God was made manifest among us, that God sent his only Son into the world, so that we might live through him" (1 John 4:9). This was His amazing provision for us fallen creatures.
- "I have loved you with an everlasting love; therefore I have continued my faithfulness to you" (Jer. 31:3). This is the work of His Spirit, by the power of His grace, by creating in you a deep need, by attracting you by His gentleness.
- "And I will betroth you to me forever. I will betroth you to me in righteousness and in justice, in steadfast love and in mercy" (Hos. 2:19). Having made us willing to give ourselves to Him, the Lord enters into an everlasting marriage contract with us.

This loving-kindness of the Lord is never removed from His children. It might appear to disappear, yet it never is. Since the Christian is in Jesus, nothing can separate him from the love of God (Rom. 8:39). God has involved Himself by covenant, and our sins cannot make it void. God has sworn that if His children do not keep His commandments He will "punish their transgression with the rod and their iniquity with stripes." Yet He adds, "but I will not remove from him my steadfast love or be false to my faithfulness. I will not violate my covenant or alter the word that went forth from my lips." (Ps. 89:31-34). See the change from *"their"* and *"them"* to *"my."* The loving-kindness of God toward His people is centered in Jesus. Because His loving-kindness is a covenant engagement; it is often linked to His truth (Ps.

40:11, 138:2), showing that it comes to us by promise. So, we should never despair.

"For the mountains may depart and the hills be removed, but my steadfast love shall not depart from you, and my covenant of peace shall not be removed, says the Lord, who has compassion on you" (Isa. 54:10). That covenant has been guaranteed by the blood of its Mediator, which has removed our sin and brought perfect reconciliation. God knows the thoughts He has for those embraced in His covenant and who have been reconciled to Him: "plans for welfare and not for evil" (Jer. 29:11).

"By day the Lord commands his steadfast love, and at night his song is with me" (Ps. 42:8). What a verse! The Lord does not just give His loving-kindness, but He commands it. It is given by decree, granted by royal engagement, as He also commands "deliverances… the blessing, life forevermore." (Ps. 44:4; 133:3), which announces that nothing can possibly stop these supplies.

Our Response

How should we respond?

1. "Therefore be imitators of God, as beloved children. And walk in love" (Eph 5:1,2). "Put on then, as God's chosen ones, holy and beloved, compassionate hearts" (Col 3:12). "For your [loving-kindness] is before my eyes, and I walk in your faithfulness" (Ps. 26:3). David loved meditating on it. It refreshed his soul and shaped his conduct. The more we are

occupied with God's goodness, the more careful we will be about our obedience. The constraints of God's love and grace are more powerful to Christians than the terrors of His Law. "How precious is your [loving-kindness], O God! The children of mankind take refuge in the shadow of your wings" (Ps. 36:7).
2. It strengthens our faith and promotes confidence in God.
3. It stimulates our worship. "Because your steadfast love is better than life, my lips will praise you" (Ps. 63:3, 138:2).
4. It is our comfort when depressed. "Let your steadfast love comfort me" (Ps. 119:76). It was with Jesus in His anguish (Ps. 69:17).
5. It should be our request in prayer, "Give me life according to your [loving-kindness]" (Ps. 119:159). David appealed to that attribute for new strength and increased energy.
6. We should appeal to it when we have backslidden. "Have mercy on me, O God, according to your [loving-kindness]" (Ps. 51:1). Deal with me according to Your gentlest attributes.
7. It should be a petition in our evening devotions. "Let me hear in the morning of your [loving-kindness]" (Ps. 143:8). Wake me up with my soul in tune, let my waking thoughts be of Your goodness.

Reflections

This is another old term that causes a bit of confusion in our modern understanding. We seldom use it, choosing to rather talk about love and kindness as distinct concepts. But this term rolls both of these into one, to describe tender and benevolent affection. It's God's incredible generosity toward us. When we least deserve it, He pours His love on us in abundance like random acts of kindness. It is unconditional, despite the nonsense we get up to and the trouble we cause. He goes over and above simple love and channels His blessings to us with kindness as well. In some newer versions of the Bible, it is translated as steadfast love that is always open to us, regardless of our circumstances or standing. It never lets go, holding on even when we turn our backs on Him!

1. Would you describe God as kind?
2. Why do we not deserve this kindness toward us?
3. What do we see of God's intentions in His acts of loving-kindness?
4. Why is Jesus such an important part of God's loving-kindness to us? Read Ephesians 2:6-7.

16

THE LOVE OF GOD

God's Nature

There are three things we see in the Bible about the nature of God.

1. "God is **spirit**" (John 4:24): In Greek, there is no indefinite article, and to say "God is a spirit" is not correct because it puts Him in a class with others. God is *"spirit"* in the highest sense. Because He is *"spirit,"* He is intangible, having no visible substance. If God had a physical body, He would not be omnipresent, He would be limited to one place. Because He is *"spirit,"* He fills heaven and earth.
2. "God is **light**" (1 John 1:5): the opposite of darkness. In the Bible, darkness represents sin, evil, and death, while *"light"* is for holiness, goodness, and life. *"God

is light" means that He is the sum of all these attributes.
3. "God is **love**" (1 John 4:8): It is not simply that God loves, but that He is Love. Love is not just one of His attributes, but His very nature.

There are many people who talk about the love of God but are total strangers to the God of love. His love is often seen as a weakness, a sort of good-natured indulgence, and is reduced to a sweet sentiment, like the human emotion. The truth is that our thoughts need to be formed and regulated by what is revealed in the Bible. This is urgently needed because of the widespread ignorance and the low state of spirituality among Christians. How little real love there is for God! One reason is that our hearts are hardly occupied with His wonderful love for His people. The more we are acquainted with His love—its character, fullness, blessedness—the more our hearts will be drawn in love to Him.

The Nature of His Love

- The love of God is **uninfluenced**. There was nothing in the recipients of His love to call it into action, nothing in us to attract or prompt it. The love which one person has for another is because of something in the person, but the love of God is free, spontaneous, and uncaused. The only reason why God loves anyone is found in His sovereign will: "It was not because you were more in number than any other people that the Lord set his love on you and chose you, for you were the fewest of all peoples, but it is because the Lord loves you" (Deut. 7:7-8). God has loved His people from everlasting, and so, nothing about the creature can be the cause of what is found in God from eternity.

He loves from Himself "because of his own purpose and grace" (2 Tim. 1:9). "We love because he first loved us" (1 John 4:19). God did not love us because we loved Him, but He loved us before we had a grain of love for Him. If God had loved us in return for ours, then it would not be spontaneous, but because He loved us when we were loveless, it is clear that His love was uninfluenced. It is very important, if God is to be honored and the hearts of His children established, that we should be clear on this truth. God's love for me and for each of His own was entirely unmoved by anything in us. What was there in me to attract the heart of God? Absolutely nothing. There was everything to repel Him, everything calculated to make Him hate me—sinful, depraved, a mass of corruption, with nothing good in me.

What was there in me that could merit esteem,

Or give the Creator delight?

'Twas even so, Father, I ever must sing,

Because it seemed good in Thy sight. (Keene, 2019)

- It is **eternal**. God is eternal, and God is love. Therefore, as God Himself had no beginning, His love had none. This concept goes beyond our feeble minds, but, where we cannot comprehend, we can bow in adoring worship. "I have loved you with an everlasting love; therefore I have continued my faithfulness to you" (Jer. 31:3). How incredible to know that the great and holy God loved His people before heaven and earth were called into existence, that He had His heart set on them from all eternity. This is proof that His love is spontaneous because He loved them ages before they had any being. "Even as he chose us in him before the foundation of the world, that we should be holy and blameless before him. In love he predestined us" (Eph. 1:4-5). This should cause His children to praise Him! How comforting for the heart: since God's love toward me had no beginning, it can have no ending! Since it is true that *"from everlasting to everlasting"* He is God, and since God is *"love,"* then it is also true that *"from everlasting to everlasting"* He loves His people.

- It is **sovereign**. God is sovereign, under no obligation to anyone, a law unto Himself, acting always according to His own pleasure. Since God is sovereign, and since He is love, it follows that His love is sovereign. Because God is God, He does as He pleases. Because God is love, He loves whom He pleases. "Jacob I loved, but Esau I hated" (Rom. 9:13). There was no reason in Jacob why he should be the object of love and not Esau. They both had the same parents and were born at the same time, being twins, yet God loved the one and hated the other! Why? Because it pleased Him to do so.

The sovereignty of God's love is not influenced by anything in people. The cause of His love lies in Himself —He loves whom He pleases. Think about the opposite. Suppose God's love was regulated by something other than His will: in such a case He would love by rule and loving by rule; He would be under a law of love, and instead of being free, God would then also be ruled by law. "In love he predestined us for adoption to himself as sons through Jesus Christ, according to"—what? Some characteristic He foresaw in them? No! So, then what? "… according to the purpose of his will" (Eph. 1:4-5).

- It is **infinite**. Everything about God is infinite. His essence fills heaven and earth. His wisdom is immeasurable because He knows everything about the past, present, and future. His power is unrestrained because there is nothing too hard for Him. So, His love is without limit. There is a depth to it that no one can fathom. There is a height to it that no one can scale. There is a length and breadth to it which defies measurement, by any human standards. It is beautifully illustrated in this verse: "But God, being rich in mercy, because of the great love with which he loved us" (Eph. 2:4). The word *"great"* is parallel with the word *"so"* in John 3:16: "God so loved." It tells us that the love of God is so superior, it cannot be estimated. John Brine (2009) out it like this:

No tongue can fully express the infinitude of God's love, or any mind comprehend it: it "surpasses knowledge" (Eph.

3:19). The most extensive ideas that a finite mind can frame about divine love, are infinitely below its true nature. Heaven is not as far above the earth as the goodness of God is beyond the most raised conceptions that we are able to form of it. It is an ocean which swells higher than all the mountains of opposition in such as are the objects of it. It is a fountain from which flows all necessary good to all those who are interested in it.

- It is **immutable**. With God, there is "no variation or shadow due to change" (Jam. 1:17), so His love knows neither change nor decrease. Jacob supplies a clear example of this: "Jacob have I loved," declared Jehovah, and despite all his unbelief and disobedience, He never ceased to love him. John 13:1 gives us another beautiful illustration. That very night one of the apostles would say, "Show us the Father," another would deny Him and all of them would forsake Him and leave. Nevertheless, "having loved his own who were in the world, he loved them to the end." God's love is subject to no variations. It is "strong as death… Many waters cannot quench love, neither can floods drown it" (Song 8:6-7). Nothing can separate us from it.

For I am sure that neither death nor life, nor angels nor rulers, nor things present nor things to come, nor powers, nor height nor depth, nor anything else in all creation, will be able to separate us from the love of God in Christ Jesus our Lord. (Rom. 8:35-39)

- It is **holy**. God's love is not ruled by impulse, passion, or emotion, but by principle. Just as His grace reigns not at the expense of it, but "through righteousness" (Rom 5:21), so His love never conflicts with His holiness. "God is light" (1 John 1:5) is mentioned before "God is love" (1 John 4:8). God's love is not some weakness or softness. The Bible declares, "For the Lord disciplines the one he loves, and chastises every son whom he receives" (Heb. 12:6). God will not turn a blind eye to sin, even in His own people. His love is pure, without any soppy sentimentality.
- It is **gracious**. The love and favor of God are inseparable. This is clearly brought out in Romans 8:32-39. That love is easily understood from the context: that generosity and grace of God which determined Him to give His Son for sinners. That love was the impulsive power of Christ's incarnation: "For God so loved the world, that he gave his only Son" (John 3:16). Christ died not to make God love us, but because He did love His people. Calvary is the supreme demonstration of divine love. Whenever you are tempted to doubt the love of God, go back to Calvary.

This is enough reason to trust and have patience in hard times. Jesus was loved by the Father, yet He was not excused from poverty, disgrace, and persecution. He was hungry and thirsty. It was not contrary to God's love for Jesus to be spit on and beaten. So, let no Christians question God's love when they go through painful afflictions and trials. God did not supplement Jesus on earth with temporary prosperity, because He had not where to lay His head. But He did give Him the Spirit without measure (John 3:34). Learn then that spiritual blessings are the gifts of God's love. How wonderful to know that when the world hates us, God loves us!

Reflections

God is love. There should be no more to say, but as humans, our emotional idea of love gets us stuck, and we end up with a skewed idea of it. We love ice cream, a good book, and God... it all gets lumped into one big, messy category. It's even worse when we are guided by our feelings. If our day is bad, then we don't feel God's love at all, and think maybe it doesn't exist. The Bible tells us He is love and does not stop being so, regardless of how we feel or what we think. It's always good to be reminded, to constantly meditate on His love as the Word shows us, so we can have a proper understanding of it.

1. What is the difference between feeling and knowing the love of God?
2. Do you see Him as more of a God of love or of justice and anger? Why?
3. How does this aspect of love set God apart from many of the gods of other religions?
4. Read Psalm 86:15. What connection does God's love have with patience, mercy, and grace?

17

THE LOVE OF GOD FOR US

By "us" we mean his people. Although we read of the love "in Christ Jesus our Lord" (Rom. 8:39), the Bible knows nothing of a love of God outside of Jesus. "The Lord is good to all, and his mercy is over all that he has made" (Ps. 145:9) so that He provides even the birds with food. "He is kind to the ungrateful and the evil" (Luke 6:35), and His provision extends to the just and the unjust (Matt. 5:45). But His love is reserved for His chosen people. Its characteristics clearly establish that, because the attributes of His love are identical with Himself. And because God is love.

His Love in Jesus

It is like saying God's love is like Himself, from everlasting to everlasting—immutable. There is nothing more absurd than to imagine that anyone loved by God can perish eternally or experience His everlasting vengeance. Since the love of God is in Jesus, it was not attracted or repelled by anything in its recipients. "Having loved his own who were in the world, he loved them to the end" (John 13:1). The *"world"* in John 3:16 is a general term that does not include the Jews, and does not contradict Psalms 5:5, 6:7; John 3:36; Romans 9:13. The main aim of God is to convey the love of God in Jesus because He is the only channel it flows through.

The Son did not persuade the Father to love His people, but it was His love for them which moved Him to give His Son for them.

Ralph Erskine (1865) said:

God has chosen a marvelous way to manifest His love. When He would show His power, He makes a world. When He would display His wisdom, He puts it in a frame and form that discovers its vastness. When He would manifest the grandeur and glory of His name, He makes a heaven, and puts angels and archangels, principalities and powers in it. And when He would manifest His love, what will He not do? God has taken a great and marvelous way of manifesting it in Christ: His person, His blood, His death, His righteousness.

"For all the promises of God find their Yes in him. That is why it is through him that we utter our Amen to God for his glory" (2 Cor. 1:20). As we were chosen in Jesus (Eph. 1:4), as we were accepted in Him (Eph. 1:6), as our life is hidden in Him (Col. 3:3), so are we loved in Him—the love of God in Christ Jesus. He is our head and husband, which is why nothing can separate us from Him, because that union is unbreakable.

His Love to Us

Nothing encourages our hearts as much as spiritually understanding God's love. When we are focused on it, we are lifted outside of and above our sinful selves. A belief fills the renewed soul with holy satisfaction and makes us as happy as we can be on this side of heaven. Knowing and believing God's love for me is a taste of heaven itself. God loves His people in Jesus, not for any good or attractive qualities about them: "Jacob have I loved." Yes, the naturally unattractive, and despicable, Jacob— "you worm Jacob" (Isa. 41:14). Since God loves His people in Jesus, it is not because of their fruitfulness, but it is always the same. Because He loves them **in** Jesus, the Father loves them **as** Jesus. The time will come when His prayer will be answered, "so that the world may know that you sent me and loved them even as you loved me" (John 17:23).

Only faith can understand those marvelous things because reasoning and feelings cannot. God loves us in Jesus. What infinite delight the Father has as He sees His people in His dear Son! All our blessings flow from that precious fountain.

God's love to His people is not of yesterday. It did not begin with their love to Him. No, "We love because he first loved us" (1 John 4:19). We do not first give to Him, so He returns to us again. Our regeneration is not the motive of His love— His love is the reason why He renews us in His image.

When I passed by you again and saw you, behold, you were at the age for love, and I spread the corner of my garment over you and covered your nakedness; I made my vow to you and entered into a covenant with you, declares the Lord God, and you became mine. (Eze. 16:8)

Not only are we at our worst when God's love is first revealed to us, but we are doing our worst, as in the case of Saul of Tarsus. Not only does God's love come before ours, but it also was birthed in His heart toward us long before we were delivered from the power of darkness and translated into the Kingdom of His dear Son. It did not begin in time but is sealed in eternity. "I have loved you with an everlasting love" (Jer. 31:3). "In this is love, not that we have loved God but that he loved us and sent his Son to be the propitiation for our sins" (1 John 4:10). It is clear from those words that God loved His people while they were naturally deprived of grace and without a grain of love toward Him or faith in Him—while they were His enemies (Rom. 5:8, 10).

That puts me under far more obligation to love, serve, and glorify Him than if He loved me for the first time when my heart was won. All the acts of God to His people are expressions of the love He had from eternity. It is because God loves us in Jesus, and has done so from everlasting, that the gifts of His love are unchangeable.

They are the gifts of "the Father of lights, with whom there is no variation or shadow due to change" (Jam. 1:17). The love of God changes us when it is "poured into our hearts," but it makes none in Him (Rom. 5:5). He sometimes changes the measure of His provision toward us, but not because His affection has altered. Even when He disciplines us, it is in love, since He has our good in mind (Heb. 12:6).

His Love in Action

Let us look more closely at some of the operations of God's love.

1. **Election**: "We ought always to give thanks to God for you, brothers beloved by the Lord, because God chose you as the first fruits to be saved, through sanctification by the Spirit and belief in the truth." (2 Thess. 2:13). There is a clear connection between God's love and choosing those who were to be saved. That election is the consequence of His love: "It was not because you were more in number than any other people that the Lord [1] set his love on you and [2] chose you" (Deut. 7:7). "In love he predestined us for adoption to himself as sons through Jesus Christ, according to the purpose of his will" (Eph. 1:4-5).
2. **Redeeming**: As we have seen from 1 John 4:10, out of His sovereign love God made a way for Jesus to take on their sins, even though He was angry because they had violated His law. "How will he not also with him graciously give us all things?" (Rom. 8:32)—another clear proof that His Son was not delivered up to the cross for all mankind. For He does not give them the Holy Spirit, a new nature, or repentance and faith.
3. **Calling**: From the Savior on the throne, the Father sends the Holy Spirit (Acts 2:33). Having loved His chosen people with an everlasting love, He draws them with loving-kindness (Jer. 31:3), gives them

newness of life, calls them out of darkness into His marvelous light, and makes them His children. "See what kind of love the Father has given to us, that we should be called children of God" (1 John 3:1). If becoming His children is not part of God's love, to what purpose are those words?
4. **Healing Backslidings**: "I will heal their apostasy; I will love them freely" (Hos. 14:4) without reluctance or hesitation. "Many waters cannot quench love, neither can floods drown it." (Song. 8:7). This is God's love to His people—invincible, unquenchable. Not only is there no possibility it will expire, but also the black waters of backsliding cannot extinguish it, nor the floods of unbelief put it out.

Nothing is more irresistible than death in the natural world, nothing so invincible as the love of God in the realm of grace.

Goodwin (2022) said:

What difficulties does the love of God overcome! For God to overcome His own heart! Do you think it was nothing for Him to put His Son to death? When He came to call us, were there no difficulties which love overcame? We were dead in trespasses and sins, yet He loved us and renewed us from the grave of our corruption. Even then did God come and conquer us. After our calling, how sadly we provoke God! Such temptations that deceive the elect. It is so with all Christians. No righteous man but he is scarcely saved (1 Peter 4:18), and yet saved he is, because the love of God is invincible: it overcomes all difficulties.

Let God's love engage your mind every day through meditations so that your heart may be drawn to Him. When your spirit is low or you are going through hardships, plead His love in prayer, knowing it cannot deny anything good for you. Make God's wonderful love the incentive of your obedience to Him—gratitude requires nothing less.

Reflections

Pink was clever enough to differentiate between God's love and His love for us. While they are very closely connected, the first is God's attribute in Himself, and the one in the chapter is more His overflow of that attribute to us. He loved us before we even considered Him, but there is more… Yes, God is love without discrimination, but His love for His chosen people, His children, is specific—not for all mankind. It sets Christians apart from the rest of the world. He loves every person, died for all, and continues to call them to Himself, but only those who are born again receive the fullness of His love in Christ.

1. What would prove God's love to you?
2. Do you sometimes struggle to understand or accept God's love for you? Why?
3. Why is it so important that God loved us before we love Him? Read 1 John 4:8-12.
4. How does God loving us affect our capacity to love ourselves and others?
5. It is good to meditate and study the Bible on this concept, but simply asking God to show you His love

is where we will begin to see it as He reveals it to us. Ask Him.

18

THE WRATH OF GOD

It is sad to find so many Christians who think the wrath of God is something they need to apologize for, or they wish it did not exist. Some do not go so far as to openly admit that they consider it a flaw in God's character, yet they do not appreciate it. They do not like to think about it, and whenever they hear it mentioned, a secret resentment rises in their hearts. Even with those who are more sober in their judgment, few imagine God's wrath as something too severe to be too terrifying to think about. Others are deluded into thinking His wrath is not consistent with His goodness, and so they dismiss it from their thoughts.

He Does Not Hide the Facts

Many turn away from God's wrath as though they were asked to look at some mistake in God's character or some imperfection in His government. But what does the Bible say? There, we find that God does not try to conceal the facts concerning His wrath. He is not ashamed to make it known that vengeance and fury belong to Him. His own challenge is:

See now that I, even I, am he,

and there is no god beside me;

I kill and I make alive;

I wound and I heal;

and there is none that can deliver out of my hand.

For I lift up my hand to heaven

and swear, As I live forever,

if I sharpen my flashing sword

and my hand takes hold on judgment,

I will take vengeance on my adversaries

and will repay those who hate me. (Deut. 32:39-41)

A study of the Bible shows that there are more verses about the anger, fury, and wrath of God than there are about His love and gentleness. Because God is holy, He hates all sin; and because He hates all sin, His anger burns against the sinner (Ps. 7:11). The wrath of God is as much an attribute as is His faithfulness, power, or mercy. There is no mistake or the slightest defect in God's character, yet there would be if wrath were absent from Him!

Indifference to sin is a moral imperfection, and anyone who does not hate it is a moral leper. How could He who is the sum of all attributes look at virtue and vice, wisdom and folly in the same way? How could He who is infinitely holy disregard sin and refuse to show His "severity" toward it? (Rom. 11:22). How could He, who delights in everything pure and lovely, not hate everything impure and wicked? The nature of God makes Hell as real a necessity, as imperatively and eternally, as Heaven is. Not only is there no imperfection in God, but there is no perfection in Him that is less perfect than another.

The wrath of God is His eternal hatred for all unrighteousness. It is His displeasure and indignation against evil. It is the holiness of God stirred into action against sin. It is the cause of the sentence He passes on evildoers. God is angry against sin because it is a rebelling against His authority, a wrong done to His sacred sovereignty. Rebels against God's government who despise His majesty and do not care about His judgment will know that God is the Lord, that His majesty is great, and how terrible His judgment is.

God's anger is not a spiteful and malicious retaliation, inflicting pain for the sake of it, or because he has been hurt. No, even though God will vindicate His authority over the universe, He will not be vindictive. His wrath is one of His perfect attributes and is not only evident from what we have just read but is also clearly established in His Word. "For the wrath of God is revealed from heaven" (Rom. 1:18). Robert Haldane (1958) comments on this verse as follows:

It was revealed when the sentence of death was first pronounced, the earth was cursed, and man was driven out of the earthly paradise, and afterward by punishments like the Flood, and the destruction of Sodom and Gomorrah by fire from heaven, but especially by the reign of death throughout the world. It was proclaimed in the curse of the law on every transgression and was implied in the ritual of sacrifice, and in all the services of Moses' Law. In Romans 8, Paul calls the attention of believers to the fact that the whole creation has become subject to vanity and groans and travails together in pain. The same creation which declares that there is a God, and publishes His glory, also proves that He is the enemy of sin and the avenger of the crimes of men... (55-56)

But above all, the wrath of God was revealed from heaven when the Son of God came down to manifest the divine character, and when that wrath was displayed in His sufferings and death in a manner more awful than by all the signs God had given before of His displeasure against sin. Besides this, the future and eternal punishment of the wicked is now declared in terms more solemn and explicit than formerly. Under the new dispensation, there are two revelations given from heaven, one of wrath, the other of grace.

The wrath of God as an attribute is clearly shown in Psalm 95:11: "Therefore I swore in my wrath." There are two occasions when God swears: in making promises (Gen. 22:16), and in pronouncing judgments (Deut. 1:34). In the first, He swears in mercy to His children; in the second, He swears to remove a wicked generation from its inheritance because of complaining and unbelief. An oath is for solemn confirmation (Heb. 6:16). In Genesis 22:16, God says, "By myself I have sworn." In Psalm 89:35 He declares, "Once for all I have sworn by my holiness." In Psalm 95:11, He affirms, "I swore in my wrath." So, Jehovah shows His wrath as an attribute equal to His holiness: He swears by the one as much as by the other! In Jesus, "the whole fullness of deity dwells bodily" (Col. 2:9), and since all the attributes are perfectly revealed in Him (John 1:18), so we read of "the wrath of the Lamb" (Rev. 6:16).

Reflecting on God's Wrath

The wrath of God is a perfection of God's character that we need to meditate on often.

1. Our hearts will know God's **hatred of sin**. We often regard sin lightly, smoothing over its ugliness and making excuses for it. But the more we study God's hatred of sin and His terrible punishment for it, the more we will realize how ugly it really is.
2. We will have a **true fear** in our souls for God. "Let us offer to God acceptable worship, with reverence and awe, for our God is a consuming fire" (Heb. 12:28-29). We cannot serve him acceptably unless there is proper *"reverence"* for His Majesty and godly fear of His righteous anger. These are realized when we remember that *"our God is a consuming fire."*
3. It will cause our souls to **fervently praise**. We should praise Him for delivering us from "the wrath to come" (1 Thess. 1:10). Our readiness or reluctance to meditate upon the wrath of God becomes a sure test of our hearts' true attitude toward Him. If we do not rejoice in God, for what He is, and because of all His attributes, then how can the love of God live in us? Each of us needs to be on our

guard against making an image of God in our thoughts that is derived from our evil preferences. The Lord complained, "You thought that I was one like yourself" (Ps. 50:21). If we do not rejoice "and give thanks to his holy name" (Ps. 97:12), if we do not rejoice to know that soon, God will reveal His wrath by taking vengeance on everyone who opposes Him; it is proof that our hearts are not in subjection to Him, that we are still in our sins, and that we are on the way to the everlasting fire.

Justice Through His Wrath

"Rejoice with him, O heavens; bow down to him, all gods, for he avenges the blood of his children and takes vengeance on his adversaries" (Deut. 32:43). And again we read:

I heard what seemed to be the loud voice of a great multitude in heaven, crying out,

"Hallelujah!

Salvation and glory and power belong to our God,

for his judgments are true and just;

for he has judged the great prostitute

who corrupted the earth with her immorality,

and has avenged on her the blood of his servants."

Once more they cried out,

"Hallelujah!

The smoke from her goes up forever and ever. (Rev 19:1-3)

On that day, Christians will rejoice when the Lord vindicates His majesty, exercises His authority, magnifies His justice, and overthrows the proud rebels who have dared to defy Him.

"If you, O Lord, should mark [impute] iniquities, O Lord, who could stand? (Ps. 130:3). We should ask this same question, because it is written, "the wicked will not stand in the judgment" (Ps. 1:5). How painfully Jesus' soul held thoughts of God marking the iniquities of His people when they were on Him! He was distressed and troubled (Mark 14:33). His awful agony, His bloody sweat, His strong cries and supplications (Heb. 5:7), His reiterated prayers—"If it be possible, let this cup pass from me" (Matt. 26:39)—His last dreadful cry —"My God, my God, why have you forsaken me?" (Matt. 27:46)—all showed what he understood of what it was for God to *mark iniquities.* So, poor sinners should cry out, "Lord, who of us can stand when the Son of God trembled beneath the weight of His wrath?"

If you have not fled for refuge to Jesus, the only Savior, "what will you do in the thicket of the Jordan?" (Jer. 12:5).

When I consider how the goodness of God is abused by most of mankind, I can only think that the greatest miracle in the world is God's patience and bounty to an ungrateful world. If a prince has an enemy in one of his towns, he does not send them provision, but lays siege to the place and does what he can to starve them. But the great God, who could wink all His enemies into destruction, bears with them and is at daily cost to maintain them. He has every right to command us to bless them that curse us if He does good for the evil and ungrateful. But do not think, sinners, that you will escape this way; God's mill goes slow but grinds small; the more admirable His patience and bounty are now, the more dreadful and insupportable that fury will be that arises out of His abused goodness. Nothing smoother than the sea, yet when stirred into a tempest, nothing rages more. Nothing so sweet as the patience and goodness of God, and nothing so terrible as His wrath when it takes fire (William Gurnall, 1660).

Then *"flee,"* my reader, flee to Jesus; "flee from the wrath to come" (Matt. 3:7) before it is too late. Do not think that this message is intended for somebody else. It is for you! Do not be content in thinking you have already fled to Christ. Make certain! Beg the Lord to search your heart and show you yourself.

Preach His Wrath

Pastors, do we preach on this subject as much as we should? The Old Testament prophets frequently told their hearers that their wicked lives provoked the Holy One of Israel and that they were gathering up wrath for themselves against the day of wrath. And conditions in the world are no better now than they were then! Nothing is so calculated to arouse the careless and cause people to search their hearts, as to preach the fact that there is a "God who feels indignation every day" for the wicked (Ps. 7:11). John the Baptist warned his hearers to "flee from the wrath to come" (Matt 3:7). The Savior told them, "Fear him who, after he has killed, has authority to cast into hell. Yes, I tell you, fear him!" (Luke 12:5). Paul said, "Therefore, knowing the fear of the Lord, we persuade others" (2 Cor. 5:11). Faithfulness demands that we speak as clearly about hell as about heaven.

Reflections

The picture of God as an angry old man wielding fire and brimstone down on unfortunate souls has become a common view in the world, as well as among Christians. Even the word "wrath" is seldom used in modern English, but when it is, it conveys only doom and gloom. As Pink says, this is one attribute most of us would rather avoid or ignore. We would rather just have a loving God who is more like Father Christmas than one who brings judgment to the earth. But the Bible is very clear that He is a God of mercy and love, but also one who is holy, and cannot simply waive away sins unless they are covered by Jesus' blood. To accept this attribute is a sobering step for every Christian, as we should always come before Him reverently and with godly fear.

1. What do wrath and judgment have to do with each other?
2. What is your view of God's wrath? Does it affect the way you approach/worship/pray to God?
3. What does the term godly fear mean?
4. How does this relate to Hebrews 4:16 which says we can approach His throne confidently, boldly, and without fear?

19

THE CONTEMPLATION OF GOD

God's Nature

In the previous chapters, we have covered some of the wonderful and lovely attributes of God's character, although it is an inadequate attempt on my part. But from these, we can see the following:

God is an **incomprehensible being**. Lost in wonder at His infinite greatness, we will use Zophar's words:

Can you find out the deep things of God?

Can you find out the limit of the Almighty?

It is higher than heaven—what can you do?

Deeper than Sheol—what can you know?

Its measure is longer than the earth

and broader than the sea. (Job 11:7-9)

When we think about God's eternity, His immateriality, His omnipresence, and His almightiness, our minds are overwhelmed.

Studying the Deity

But the complexity of His nature is no reason to stop inquiring and trying to understand what He has so graciously revealed of Himself in His Word. Because we are unable to have perfect knowledge, it would be silly to say we will make no effort at all to gain some understanding. Charles Spurgeon (n.d.) said:

Nothing will so enlarge the intellect, nothing so magnify the whole soul of man, as a devout, earnest, continued, investigation of the great subject of the Deity. The most excellent study for expanding the soul is the science of Christ and Him crucified and the knowledge of the Godhead in the glorious Trinity.

Another quote from this prince of preachers:

The proper study of the Christian is the Godhead. The highest science, the loftiest speculation, the mightiest philosophy, which can engage the attention of a child of God is the name, the nature, the person, the doings, and the existence of the great God which he calls his Father. There is something exceedingly improving to the mind in a contemplation of the Divinity. It is a subject so vast, that all our thoughts are lost in its immensity; so deep, that our pride is drowned in its infinity. Other subjects we can comprehend and grapple with; in them we feel a kind of self-contentment, and go on our way with the thought, "Behold I am wise." But when we come to this master science, finding that our plumbline cannot sound its depth, and that our eagle eye cannot see its height, we turn away with the thought, "I am but of yesterday and know nothing." (Sermon on Mal. 3:6)

Yes, the complexity of His nature should teach us humility, caution, and reverence. After all our searching and meditation, we can say, "Behold, these are but the outskirts of his ways, and how small a whisper do we hear of him!" (Job 26:14). When Moses asked Jehovah to see His glory, God answered, "[I] will proclaim before you my name 'The Lord'" (Ex. 33:19). His name is the collection of His attributes.

John Howe (1822) said:

The idea we can form of His glory is only as much as we can have of a large book by a brief synopsis, or of a spacious country by a little landscape painting. He has given us a true report of Himself, but not in full; enough to secure our understanding, to guide us from error, but not from ignorance. We can apply our minds to contemplate the several perfections whereby the blessed God reveals His being to us and in our thoughts attribute them all to Him, though we have still but low and defective conceptions of each one. Yet so far as our apprehensions can correspond to the discovery that He allows us of His several excellencies, we have a present view of His glory.

The difference between the knowledge of God we have in this life and the one we will have in Heaven is huge, but the one we have now should not be undervalued because it is imperfect, and we must not magnify the second one above its reality. The Bible does say we will see "face to face" *and* "know" even as we are known (1 Cor. 13:12). But to assume that we will then know God as fully as He knows us is to be misled by the sound of words, and to disregard the limits of that knowledge. There is a vast difference between us being glorified and us being made divine. In our glorified state, we as Christians will still be finite creatures, and therefore, never able to fully comprehend the infinite God.

The saints in heaven will see God with the eye of the mind, for He will be always invisible to the physical eye. They will see Him more clearly than they could see Him by reason and faith, and more extensively than all His works and dispensations had hitherto revealed Him. But their minds will not be so enlarged as to be capable of contemplating at once, or in detail, the whole excellence of His nature. To comprehend infinite perfection, they must become infinite themselves. Even in Heaven, their knowledge will be partial, but at the same time, their happiness will be complete because their knowledge will be perfect in this sense, that it will be adequate to the capacity of the subject, although it will not exhaust the fullness of the object. We believe that it will be progressive and that as their views expand, their blessedness will increase. But it will never reach a limit beyond which there is nothing to be discovered, and when ages after ages have passed away, He will still be the incomprehensible God (Dick, 1840).

God is an **all-sufficient Being**. He is all-sufficient in Himself and to Himself. As the first of beings, He could receive nothing from another, nor be limited by the power of another. Being infinite, He possesses all possible perfection. When the Trinity existed all alone, He was everything to Himself. His understanding, love, and energy found an adequate recipient in Himself. If He needed anything external, He would not have been independent and would not have been God. He created all things for Himself (Col. 1:16), but it was not to fill a lack, but that He might transmit life and happiness to angels and men and show them His glory. He demands the allegiance and service of His intelligent creatures, but He gains no benefit from their duties—the advantage is for themselves (Job 22:2-3).

He uses different ways and channels to accomplish His goals, not because He has no power, but because His power is better displayed through the weakness of His instruments.

Better Than Life

God's all-sufficiency makes Him the supreme object to be sought. True happiness is only found in the enjoyment of God. His favor is life, and His loving-kindness is better than life. "'The Lord is my portion,' says my soul, 'therefore I will hope in him'" (Lam. 3:24). His love, grace, and glory are the main objects of our desire and the source of our highest satisfaction.

There are many who say, "Who will show us some good?

Lift up the light of your face upon us, O Lord!"

You have put more joy in my heart

than they have when their grain and wine abound. (Ps. 4:6-7)

Then we can say:

Though the fig tree should not blossom,

nor fruit be on the vines,

the produce of the olive fail

and the fields yield no food,

the flock be cut off from the fold

and there be no herd in the stalls,

yet I will rejoice in the Lord;

I will take joy in the God of my salvation. (Hab. 3:17-18)

The God of Creation

God is the **supreme sovereign of the universe**. We can see this best in John Dick's words:

No dominion is so absolute as that which is founded on creation. He who might not have made anything had a right to make all things according to His own pleasure. In the exercise of His uncontrolled power, He has made some parts of the creation mere inanimate matter, of lesser or more refined texture, and distinguished by different qualities, but all inert and unconscious. He has given organization to other parts, and made them susceptible to growth and expansion, but still without life in the proper sense of the term. To others, He has not only given organization but conscious existence, organs of sense and self-motive power. To these, He has given man the gift of reason, and an immortal spirit, by which he is allied to a higher order of beings who are placed in the superior regions. Over the world which He has created, He sways the scepter of omnipotence.

I blessed the Most High, and praised and honored him who lives forever,

for his dominion is an everlasting dominion,

and his kingdom endures from generation to generation;

all the inhabitants of the earth are accounted as nothing,

and he does according to his will among the host of heaven

and among the inhabitants of the earth;

and none can stay his hand

or say to him, "What have you done?" (Daniel 4:34-35)

A creature has no rights. It can demand nothing from its Maker; and in whatever manner it is treated, it has no right to complain. Yet, when thinking of the absolute dominion of God over all, we should never lose sight of His moral attributes. God is just and good and always does what is right. Nevertheless, He exercises His sovereignty according to His imperial and righteous pleasure. He assigns each creature its place as it seems good in His sight. He orders the different circumstances of each according to His own counsel. He molds each vessel according to His own uninfluenced determination. He has mercy on whom He will and hardens whom He will.

Wherever we are, His eye is on us. Whoever we are, our life, and everything is at His disposal. To the Christian, He is a tender Father; to the rebellious sinner, He will be a consuming fire. "To the King of the ages, immortal, invisible, the only God, be honor and glory forever and ever. Amen" (1 Tim. 1:17).

Reflections

God has so many facets, so many attributes, that we can easily see only one side of Him or get stuck seeing Him in only one light. But Pink's encouragement is to begin contemplating and viewing God in His fullness (or as much as possible). Christians have become too lazy or selective in how they approach and worship God. But if we want to grow, we need to allow Him to reveal Himself to us in His many different characteristics. On our part, this means having an open heart, without preconceived ideas. It means studying His Word more thoroughly to find out what He says about Himself. It means praying and listening so He can speak and tell us about who He really is.

1. How often do you think or study who God is?
2. Which of the attributes in this book was an eye-opener for you?
3. Why do you think we as Christians have such a shallow and narrow view of God?
4. What are the benefits of seeing God in His fullness? How will that impact other areas of your Christian work?

ABOUT A. W. PINK

Arthur Walkington Pink was born in 1886 into a faithful Christian household. Little is known of his upbringing, except that he studied music as part of his education. However, as a young man, his penchant for searching for the truth pushed him into the Theosophical Society, an occultic group. He rose in the secret ranks to become a prominent leader. But in 1908, he was struck by the simplicity of Proverbs 14:12: "There is a way that seems right to a man, but its end is the way to death." After three days of locking himself in his room, he emerged reborn, proclaiming Christ as his savior.

Two years later, he began studying at the Moody Bible College, but, unsatisfied with the teaching, left after only six weeks to take up a position as pastor in a Congregational church. His views, though, contradicted their doctrines, especially when it came to baptism, and he left to serve in a Baptist Church in Los Angeles. He would move around a lot during the next few years, from the US to Australia, and finally settling in the UK. During this time, he met and married Vera Russel in 1916.

His pro-Calvinist views often rubbed people up the wrong way, as well as his critical personality, and it made it difficult for him to last long in any one church. It was his writing that soon became the focus of his ministry. While he held posts in different places, he continued to be a strong proponent of the truths taught in the Bible, with over 2,000 articles and a number of books to his name.

During his stay in California, he began work on his monthly journal, *Studies in the Scriptures,* an expository of the Bible that would last until his death. His book, *The Attributes of God,* comes from those periodicals. Although he was relatively unknown at the time of his death in 1953, because of his anti-Arminianism, his fame as a biblical teacher came to the fore when certain ministers began taking notice of his writings. A major shift toward Calvinistic theology took place, and his work was immediately highlighted. One pastor even told his friends to ignore other well-known authors and simply "Read Pink" (Murray, 2004). His most famous publication, *The Sovereignty of God,* has since become one of the top Christian books after it was republished in 1961.

Richard P. Belcher (Murray, 2004) said of him:

We do not idolize him. But we do recognize him as a very unique man of God who can teach us through his pen and through his life. He was truly born to write and all the circumstances of his life, even the negative ones he did not understand, propelled him to the fulfillment of that God-ordained purpose.

BIBLIOGRAPHY

Bishop, G. S. (1912). *Grace in Galatians: A New and Concise Commentary on the Epistle*. Gospel Publishing House.

Booth, Abraham. (1803). *The Reign of Grace*.

Brine, John. (2009). *The Certain Efficacy of the Death of Christ, Asserted (1743)*.

Charnock, S. (1840). *Discourses Upon the Existence and Attributes of God*. Robert Carter and Brothers.

Charnock, S. (2023, May 14). *God's holiness*. The Puritan Board. https://www.puritanboard.com/threads/gods-holiness-stephen-charnock.111254/

Cowper, W. (n.d.). *God Moves in a Mysterious Way*. Hymnary.org. https://hymnary.org/text/god_moves_in_a_mysterious_way

Crossway. (2001). *English Standard Version Bible*. Crossway Bibles.

Dick, John. (2021). *Lectures on theology*. Monergism. https://www.monergism.com/thethreshold/sdg/dick/Lectures%20on%20Theology%20-%20John%20Dick.pdf

Edwards, Jonathan. (2024). *Jonathan Edwards: Works of Jonathan Edwards, volume two*. Ccel.org. https://ccel.org/ccel/edwards/works2.xi.iii.html

Erskine, R. (1865). *Erskine's Sermons and Practical Works*. William Tegg.

Goodwin, Thomas. (2022). *The riches of God's love to his elect*. Bibleportal.com. https://bibleportal.com/sermon/Thomas-Goodwin/the-riches-of-god-s-love-to-his-elect

Haldane, R. (1958). *Exposition of the Epistle to the Romans*. MacDonald Publishing Company.

Harvey, James. (1819). *Whole Works of the Late Rev. James Hervey*. J & M Robertson.

Holman Bible Publishers. (2016). *The Holy Bible: NKJV New King James Version*. Holman Bible Publishers.

Howe, John. (1822). *The Whole Works of Rev. John Howe*. F.Westley. http://www.digitalpuritan.net/Digital%20Puritan%20Resources/Howe%20John/The%20Whole%20Works%20of%20John%20Howe%20(vol.2).pdf

Keene, R. (2019). *Distinguishing Grace*. Hymnary.org. https://hymnary.org/text/in_songs_of_sublime_adoration_and_praise

Murray, I. H. (2004). *The Life of Arthur W. Pink*. Banner of Truth.

Musselman, John. (2023, September 15). *The Goodness of God*. Jackson Institute. https://tji.org/goodness-of-god/

Pink, A. W. (1962). *The Attributes of God*. Fig.

Spurgeon, C. (n.d.). *Charles Spurgeon on the subject of God - Resources*. Eternal Perspective Ministries. https://www.epm.org/resources/2010/Mar/12/charles-spurgeon-subject-god/

Spurgeon, C. H. (2024a). *God's Sovereignty: A Comfort to His Children*. Monergism.com. https://www.monergism.com/gods-sovereignty-comfort-his-children

Spurgeon, C. H. (2024b). *Treasury of David: Psalm 118*. Spurgeon.org. https://archive.spurgeon.org/treasury/ps118.php

"The parts of me that used to think I was different or smarter or whatever, almost made me die."

— David Foster Wallace

"People fear death even more than pain. It's strange that they fear death. Life hurts a lot more than death. At the point of death, the pain is over.
Yeah, I guess it is a friend."

— Jim Morrison

"A book is a suicide postponed."

— Emil Cioran

Acknowledgements

"The Bridge Crossing"
 — in *Drifting Sands Haibun* [USA]

"Hazards of New Fortune"
 — in *Lily Poetry Review* [USA]

"Suicide Odyssey"
 — in *Cerasus Poetry Review* [England]

"The Suicide Surrogate Confesses"
 — in *Pennsylvania Literary Journal* [USA]

"Jim Morrison Reads Poetry in Pere Lachaise Cemetery"
 — in *Samjoko Magazine* [South Korea]

In memory of Joseph LoSchiavo [1943-1977]

"Suicide might not be the most promising subject for a poetry booklet, but LindaAnn LoSchiavo's poems—both in verse and in prose—compellingly address both the fascination and the tragedy of self-extinction. These poems deal with actual suicides, whether it be among LoSchiavo's own family or celebrated figures such as Jim Morrison. But it is the obscurer individuals who have chosen to end their lives that seem to attract the poet's deepest interest and sympathy, and she skillfully weaves a tapestry of horror and pathos around these cases so that we can all feel what it is to face the awesome presence of death. " — S. T. Joshi, Editor-in-Chief, *Spectral Realms*

"A brave and insightful collection. LindaAnn approaches a subject that is often considered taboo with an erudite and eclectic collection of poems that challenge our prejudices, and cultural assumptions about death and suicide." — John Stocks, Poetry Editor, Bewildering Stories Magazine

"Felones de Se packs a lifetime of impact into six sad and darkly beautiful poems. LoSchiavo's words will stick with me for a long time. Don't miss this wonderful book of poetry." — Sonora Taylor, award-winning author of "Little Paranoias: Stories"

Contents

Tuesdays with the Ghost	2
The Bridge Crossing	4
Hazards Of New Fortune	7
Suicide Odyssey	13
The Suicide Surrogate Confesses	19
About the Author	23

LindaAnn LoSchiavo

Illustrator: Erin Caldwell

Tuesdays with the Ghost

Some rituals might be afraid to die.

You're *here* allowing emptiness to do
doom's work, reminding me emotions, rage,
regrets continue in the afterlife,
kinship's bond scarred like walls where family
portraits, removed, left ugly holes behind.

Your shoulder shrug's suspicious silhouette –
felled untried wings – had been inherited
from grandpa, whose Aeolian nature
had cultivated fortitude, aware
volcanic force can be a ruinous god.

Some rituals, like Sicily, run dry.

Inviting death to a staring contest, you
assumed the posture of a guillotine,
betting against the beauty of your life,
daring it to expire – or to apply
a tourniquet, compress pain's blood red rain.

Our weekly ritual survived, stood by.

We'd meet for lunch on Tuesdays holding hands
en route, which calmed you after therapy,
New York's vehicular va-room our song.

During one meal, amid those chin-cupped sighs,
forlornness wrote dark scripture down your back.

You'd just seen Mauna Loa's volcano.
A flirty guide lured you to the gift shop.
With his communion on your lips, you bought
a hideous Hawaiian souvenir,
you're cursed to wear in perpetuity.

Cute hula girl, displayed on red shantung,
saluting tiki gods, mid-dance, alone:

Was she your last embrace, strained neck tied, noosed,
as hula girl surveyed the upturned chair?

You did not call me on your way to ash
as angst unbuttoned from the terrified
fist your heart had become, swung loose, released.

Today is Tuesday – but no lunch is served.

You can't escape woe's blacked out page because
my memory's the urn I'll store you in.

— —

Note: Joseph LoSchiavo, who ended his life in 1977, is buried in Green-Wood Cemetery, Brooklyn, NY.

The Bridge Crossing

Suicidal dreams suspend questions of the night. Saudi sisters adrift in New York, darkness rowing them to sinister emirates. Penniless. Sorrow transported them to a souk where they barter, trading hunger for another afternoon in America. Fraught memories they finger like worry beads. A close-mouthed sky spits on the indigent. Dirty pigeons point to the river. They've become feathers, light in the arms of kismet.

> gold and copper foliage release
> the brittle branch with a whispered sigh
> floating to meet the earth's
> patchwork carpet
> their fate fulfilled

Staten Island Ferry. Accusing north winds whip open coats like a Customs Officer. The sixteen-year-old sister imagines gliding through the tide of clasped hands to a safe haven. Liberty's torch reminds the twenty-three-year-old sister of Aladdin's lamp, a jinni armed with wishes. Then a breeze strips a discarded sandwich of its wrapper. Like terns, these two foreigners scavenge for crusts. Ahead seagulls forage for food, squawking rude reminders like impertinent desk clerks.

>   catching sight
>
>   of bleary-eyed reflections
>
>   in the hotel's cheval glass
>
>   they forgot
>
>   the emptiness beneath

Central Park. Facing east, they perform *Salah*. Women walk dogs, shiny dark hair free as a raven's wings, legs bare unlike daughters of their desert homeland, always petitioning men for assent. Decisions will fly tonight, inked on postcards, explaining why return is impossible. Manhattan's mud-tinged sky is brightening to blue. They walk uptown, guided by the path of Bow Bridge as ducks quack complaints. *Still here?*

>   doves nesting
>   at the lake's edge
>   knitting a new home
>   out of trash
>   and exhausted leaves

George Washington Bridge. Unadorned steel. A domesticated red lighthouse squats at its base not unlike crusaders' tombs, faithful stone pets guarding the foot. Warm weather wrestles with their heavy coats, rocks buried in pockets. Makeshift shrouds. Winds stir undependable shadows as they ascend, dare nervous legs to reach a high ledge. A dramatic draping is left to the older sibling. Consigning their sisterhood to the pledge of duct-tape, they jump in tandem. Submerged and gone, momentary mermaids, their mighty splash a proclamation.

> boats glide over swells
> dusk darkening the Hudson River
> waves rolling off their backs
> late autumn chill gathering power
> approaching day of the dead

— —

Note: Saudi sisters Rotana Farea, 23, and Tala Farea, 16, were found on the rocky banks of the Hudson River, duct-taped to each other. Bound together, they had jumped off the George Washington Bridge. Police discovered their bodies on October 24, 2018.

Hazards Of New Fortune

Fortune

"Every disadvantage has its advantage." — Ukrainian proverb
"Kozhen nedolik maye svoyu perevahu." — Ukrainian translation

They quit the Ukraine for America, sacred place of new beginnings. Rescuing a forsaken candy shop with workman's grit, the foreigners stretched meager savings like taffy, pining for sweet success. Wrap-around windows shed sunlight on Slavic menus, neatly folded by the oldest daughter. A famous East Village poet dined here often and lured others. Full bellies fast-friended the cash register. Yet manual labor and servility felt lowly as a casual betrayal even as New York repainted their family portrait in greenbacks and gold. At closing time, each customer was tumbled out, like a salt shaker, which magically refilled, then emptied out again. Poised on a chair, the father hung a framed crisp dollar bill next to a crucifix, another object of worship.

                          daily chores
   doubled the weight   born of
                    waiting

New

"Flies will not land on a boiling pot." — *Ukrainian proverb*
"Na kyplyachu kastrulyu mukhy ne sidayut'."— *Ukrainian translation*

New profits parlayed into a real estate portfolio; deeds fingered like dominos. The novice restaurateurs sipped life lazily through a straw of wealth, the holy liturgy of labor now handed off to helpers. After the last patrons left, most of the chairs were up-ended. Across the only round table, the youngest daughter spread a starched lace cloth and the family supped together on smoked kielbasa, fried cabbage, challah bread, boiled potatoes, picking the diced carrots from the borscht to eat one at a time like golden pills — as if to protect themselves from what would come.

polished silverware
family gathers
mouths open as eyes close

Of

"The devil always takes back his gifts."— Ukrainian proverb
"Dyyavol zavzhdy zabyraye svoyi dary."— Ukrainian translation

Of a day unlike the rest. Of a sky cutting itself open, bleeding dawn's red fingers along the wall. Of an unbearable pressure. Of air spawning pearls of sweat. Of a terror gliding through squares of daylight on the bedroom floor. Of a father struggling to sit up, watching blankets rise as if winged. Of unanswered prayers to his household saints. Of final utterings unheard from his fifty-year-old mouth. Of wondering why, a bedside chair refused to support his weight as a black confusion blots out morning. Of inner momentum shorted out.

blue-shadowed cue
stilling life's hum
last breath

Hazards

"Fire starts with sparks." — *Ukrainian proverb*
"Vohon' pochynayet'sya z iskor." — *Ukrainian translation*
After the burial, the only son tried on his father's shoes. His real estate inheritance flashed like a radioactive raincoat. Maybe no one else was willing to be Judas, voting for the murder of reasonable stewardship. The dark mountain within beckoned him to climb, to gamble. He graphed his greed on their tenants' gas lines, illegally siphoned from a ground floor café. Inspectors had dismantled unlawful taps and valves, imposed fines. But impatience choked up. Winding his wickedness like a time-bomb, he offered penny-pinching menace to his mother like today's special. Fired up frenzy of milking the portfolio grew hotter until his heart heeded nothing else. One afternoon, sudden sparks shocked the basement boiler, then fireballed, torched two tenements, snuffed out lives. A swift arrest flattened the son's future like a giant's rolling pin, fried his feeble alibi, pulverized his face on the cold docket of public shame. Aware his life wouldn't balance this debt for disgusted jurors, he hailed a taxi to his next hellscape, leaving behind a note for Mama next to an upturned chair. Moments before the rope crunched his windpipe, he looked out a window imaging flames — all those faces waiting to be saved.

    red slash   explosion's
                crescendo —
      one ending and then another

Note: This East Village (NYC) gas explosion happened on Thursday, March 26, 2015

Suicide Odyssey

"You will come to the Sirens, who enchant all who venture near them."
The Odyssey, Book XII — by Homer (Samuel Butler, translator)

Mariner, 18 years old

Trauma's perpetual wine-dark sea surge
rocked him awake. Depression's ancient curse
hung like an albatross, atonement's cross.

Though born a navigator, wars he fought
began at home. It's said seafaring blood
casts boys adrift — but inner misery
misled his compass, made him run aground.

Tethered in dry dock, he untied some knots,
was certified a captain! Hired for tours!
High on the oars of feeling, bliss comes — fades
away when melancholy takes the wheel,
as if joy's ballast rolled, washed overboard.

Gloom's pirates placed glad's gold on a ghost ship,
his epic struggle baffling, unexplained.

Siren, 17 years old

A drowning man was irresistible.

Awaiting high tide, bird-disguised, she flew,
convinced lost, star-crossed sailors rescues near.

Fine-tuning flutters in her throat, she sang
notes that transmitted secret menaces.
Her voice, mysterious, entangled, lured.

Two-faced enchantress: how well she deceives.
Pretending to assist, her guile protects
him from all possibility of good.
Suicide Odyssey   [continued
with a stanza break]

Surrender

His mind's opponent was fate's nameless weight,
an anchor forged of fright, unheard distress.
Confused, diminished by its siren call,
he spread his soul on her lap like a shawl.

Maelstrom, July 13, 2014

The truck. Hesitancy.
Ignition switch. Noxious exhaust.
Coughing. Protestations.
The truck. The stench.
A rising wave of doubts.

        Ping! Ping!
            "Get back in the truck!"

Ambivalence. No, no. Wait. No.
Fear filling his nostrils.
His mariner dreams sinking.
Black carbon monoxide stinging.
The truck, floating in fumes.
Whirlpool. Dizzy with distortion.
Mermaids manning the rocks.
Scylla's six maws seething, spewing.
Charybdis shaming, cursing.
Sucking him into the maelstrom.

        Ping! Ping!
      "You just have to do it."
    Texts. Orders. Messages.
            Ping! Ping! Ping!
          Do it*! Do it like you said!"*

Then the sun resting its warm cheek
on the horizon's bright guillotine.
The truck rocking, sinking.
Toxic fumes garlanding his head.

    Ping! Ping!
      "Die! I love you."

— —

Note: Conrad Henri Roy III [12 September 1995—13 July 2014] killed himself with encouragement from Michelle Carter, 17, whose trial was known as the "texting suicide case." Texts used here were shown during the trial in Massachusetts to the jurors.

The Suicide Surrogate Confesses

Perhaps she wished to mimic opera's
iconic heroines, envisioning
this love as indispensable yet doomed.

Tonight, he called, insisting he'll commit
to it. He'll kill himself — he really will.

As usual, she was encouraging.

Then he had second thoughts. He couldn't breathe
the toxic fumes. Why not phone the police?
Or notify his family? Instead
she argued with him: "Get back in the truck!"

Obeying her commands, his body wrapped
around the nameless weight his life became,
afraid no longer of its siren song.

His absence filled his parents' pain-brain, torched
those memories of suicide attempts.
His girlfriend took his life away from them.

Demanding justice, they watched screens replay
text messages debating the ideal
method for meeting death successfully.

"Sorry I let you do this," she confessed.

After the verdict's read, the gavel pounds
the desk for order — and lifts satisfied.

Felones de Se

The suicide of Conrad Henri Roy III [1995—2014], with encouragement from his long-distance girlfriend, 17-year-old Michelle Carter, was the subject of a noted investigation and involuntary manslaughter trial in Bristol County, Massachusetts, known as the "texting suicide case." Carter was sentenced to serve 15 months in Bristol County Jail.

Jim Morrison Reads Poetry in Pere Lachaise Cemetery

"I can summon the dead." — Jim Morrison, "Power," 1969
Jim Morrison, performer, lyricist:
skewed skeleton of concert fame became
his bones, its fascinating armature
attracting tourists who'll mythologize
the self-destructive "Lizard King" who died
addicted to escaping humdrum's thrum,
buffets of opiates, the open bar
always available to young rock stars.

> His anthem: "Come on, baby, take a chance."

Jim's following now congregates around
his tomb, participates in photo opps,
attends his grand, eternal wake, laments
not getting in to The Doors' sold-out shows.

> "The end of nights we tried to die," sang Jim.

Twilight, when visitors have danced away,
Jim's ghost recites his poetry — free verse—
to literati inside Pere Lachaise:
Colette, Moliere, Gertrude Stein, Oscar Wilde.

> "Some are born to the endless night," wrote Jim.

Reclining on his slab, enjoying lines
of rhyme —because a boneyard lacks *cocaine* —
his spirit contemplates sobriety.

His Dionysian, bare-chested side,
arrested for indecent exposure,
calmed, he's aware his bathtub finale
was the last splash he'd snorted up to make.

— —

Note: Jim Morrison died, age 27, on July 3, 1971 in Paris. He started the rock group The Doors.

About the Author

LindaAnn LoSchiavo

Native New Yorker LindaAnn LoSchiavo is a member of The Science Fiction Poetry Association, The British Fantasy Society, and The Dramatists Guild. Four times a Pushcart Prize nominee, her poetry has also received nominations for Best of the Net, the Rhysling Award, and Dwarf Stars. Recently, she was PoetrySuperHighway's Poet of the Week and a finalist in Thirty West Publishing Company's "A Fresh Start" contest. Her poetry titles include the Elgin Award winner "A Route Obscure and Lonely," "Concupiscent Consumption," "Women Who Were Warned," Firecracker Award, Balcones Poetry Prize, Quill and Ink, and IPPY Award nominee "Messengers of the Macabre: Hallowe'en Poems" [co-written with David Davies], "Apprenticed to the Night" [Beacon Books, 2023], and "Felones de Se: Poems about Suicide" [Ukiyoto Publishing, 2023].

Twitter: @Mae_Westside
YouTube:
https://www.youtube.com/channel/UCHm1NZIlTZybLTFA44 wwdfg

About the Illustrator

Erin Caldwell, a painter and graphic artist from North Carolina, has a passion for bringing history and ghost stories to life on the page. *http://erinsart4.godaddysites.com*

www.ingramcontent.com/pod-product-compliance
Lightning Source LLC
LaVergne TN
LVHW020434070526
838199LV00031B/620/J